From the first moment he set foot in Canada,

MALAK KARSH

developed a strong and passionate relationship with his adopted
home; a relationship that lasted a lifetime and that shone through
every breathtaking photograph he took of this land.

THE RIGHT HONOURABLE JEAN CHRÉTIEN
NOVEMBER 8, 2001

TULIPS

FACTS AND FOLKLORE ABOUT THE WORLD'S MOST PLANTED FLOWER

PHOTOGRAPHS BY
Malak

TEXT BY
Sonia Day

KEY PORTER BOOKS

National Library of Canada Cataloguing in Publication Data

Malak
    Tulips : facts and folklore about the world's most planted flower

ISBN 1-55263-341-1

1. Tulips. 2. Tulips—History. 3. Tulips—Pictorial works. I. Day, Sonia II. Title.

SB413.T9M34 2002   635.9'3432   C2001-904278-7

Quotations were taken from the following books: Thalassa Cruso, *The Gardening Year*, published 1983 by Van Nostrand; Lauren Springer, *The Undaunted Garden*, published 1994 by Fulcrum Books. All photos by Malak with the exception of the following:
    p. 13 Topkapi Palace Museum; p. 28 Wallace Collection, London; p. 30 Kremsmunster Abbey, Upper Austria; p. 41 (top) New York Historical Society, USA/The Bridgeman Art Library; p. 72 (top); p. 73 (top); p. 82 (top); pp. 106–107; p. 114 © The International Bulb Centre, Holland; p. 88, p. 105 © Sonia Day.

Cover design: Peter Maher
Electronic formatting: Jack Steiner

Printed and bound in Canada

02 03 04 05 06 07 6 5 4 3 2 1

Contents

Introduction

I love tulips. But I didn't always. In fact, I was once a bit scared of them.

My grandmother grew tulips in her garden in Kent, England. As a small child I remember investigating one particularly fat, red bloom, curious to find out what it contained. I peeled back a couple of petals—then recoiled in fright. For lurking inside was a big black spider.

Or so I thought. What I had discovered, in reality, was simply the stamens and stigma of the tulip (which do, indeed, look a bit tarantula-like

FAMED EXPORT: Loved around the world, most tulips have their beginnings in Holland's spectacular bulb fields.

in some varieties). With no adult around to point out my error, I decided I'd better start giving Nana's favorite flowers a wide berth.

Later, as a young adult in the 1960s, I recall actively disliking tulips. They always seemed to be planted in regimented rows, in public parks, and they struck me as banal and boring. Not worth a second glance. Like many people, I had to wait till middle age— the stage in our lives when most of us get interested in garden- ing—to discover their charms. I bought a few

TARANTULA-LIKE: The innards of some tulips resemble spiders—and they once scared the author.

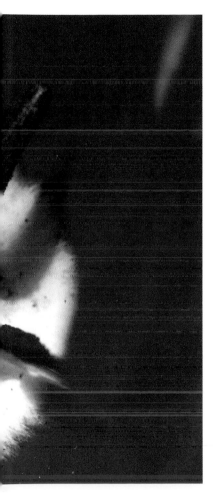

ordinary tulips, in red and white, planted them in my little city garden—and got hooked. It amazed me then (and still does) how tulips pop out of the bare flower bed in spring, so fresh and perfect-looking, after being frozen solid for months under the snow.

I've become even more enamored of tulips in the course of writing this book, for they come in so many different guises, and accompanying them is a wealth of fascinating history that's probably unmatched in the botanical world. Indeed, once you start researching tulips, it's hard to stop; the colorful stories go on and on. Included in this book are some of those stories. I hope you will find them as entertaining as I did.

one

The Tulip's Romantic Past: Turkish Harems and Impressionist Paintings

It is hard to imagine life without tulips.

In the twenty-first century, tulips are probably the world's most planted, and familiar, flower. Even people who dislike anything to do with gardening know what tulips look like. Available in a staggering 2,600-plus varieties, they have become our introduction to summer, eagerly awaited in countries ranging from the U.S. to Sweden

INSTANTLY RECOGNIZABLE: Tulips (shown here with hyacinths) are the world's most planted flowder and adored by many as a harbinger of summer.

SILENT BEAUTY: *A fountain—and singing birds—are the only things you're likely to hear in Holland's Keukenhof Gardens. Radios are banned, so that visitors can admire the flowers in peace.*

to Australia. From April onwards, in northern climates, tulips are the sight that reinvigorates us: tall, straight stems, mostly with cup-shaped flowers, popping up from flower beds in public parks and people's gardens—for there is hardly a gardener anywhere who doesn't find the space to squeeze in at least a handful of tulips.

Bending together in the wind, great swaths of these bulbous beauties look like flags outside the United Nations. Grown in clumps in a garden, they are a feast for the eyes after the gray monotony of winter. Cut and arranged indoors, in a vase, their sculptured shapes bring a touch of class to any room.

Pink tulips; yellow tulips; tulips in ten shades of red; tulips with sassy stripes; tulips as dark as the night sky or as white as freshly fallen snow; tulips with crazy, frilly petals; tulips shaped like Grecian urns; apricot-colored tulips that smell tantalizingly of honey and cloves; tulips that have funny mottled leaves; stubby tulips that sprawl along the ground, their blooms shaped like stars; tiny tulips, like little gems—when it comes to tulips, there is something to satisfy everyone.

BIG FAN: *Turkish sultans like Suleyman the Magnificent filled their harems with dancing girls and tulips.*

Universally desired and admired, tulips are a taken-for-granted treat, as anticipated and pleasurable as an ice cream cone on a hot summer afternoon. But it wasn't always so. In bygone days, these flowers inspired not just sentiment, but gut-wrenching passion. They were celebrated in Persian legends of love, and in the *Rubáiyát* of Omar Khayyám. They inspired Monet's most famous paintings. Victorian poets like Robert Browning

'Mid the sharp short emerald wheat, scarce risen three fingers well,
The wild tulip, at end of its tube, blows out its great red bell
Like a thin clear bubble of blood, for the children to pick and sell.

—Robert Browning, "Up at a Villa—Down in the City"

wrote mushy verses about them. They even saved the life of a British war correspondent, Beverley Nichols. (While being transported on a stretcher, deathly ill, through a mountainous region of India in 1939, Nichols spotted tulips growing wild, became enraptured, and decided that he wanted to live after all.) During a tumultuous time in their history—the much-ballyhooed era that's become known as Tulipomania—these remarkable flowers were so idolized and lusted after, they drove ordinary Dutch businessmen to suicide.

No one really knows when, or where, our love affair with the tulip began. Tulip designs have been found on pottery jars dating as far back as 2200 to 1600 BC, but neither the Greeks nor the Romans ever mentioned the flower in their writings. An illuminated bible from the twelfth century contains tulip motifs, but no other clues. *T. sharoniensis*, or the Sharon tulip, is thought to be "the rose of Sharon" mentioned in the Song of Solomon.

The people of Persia (now Iran) certainly knew about tulips, for they were fond of relating a *Romeo and Juliet* type of tragedy that centered on the flower. In this legend, a callow youth named Farhad falls in love with the fair maid Shirin. He rides his horse over a cliff to his death after hearing that she has been killed. (She hasn't—a rival has misled him.) On the spot where Farhad died needlessly, scarlet tulips start springing up—one flower for each drop of blood spilled on the ground. As a result, red tulips became the symbol of passionate love in ancient Persia.

Whether Persians actually grew tulips is open to debate. (They probably simply admired them in the wild.) However, one thing seems certain: the tulip did become the first flower to be cultivated solely for its beauty.

Until that time, the concept of growing things for their aesthetic value alone didn't exist. There were no "gardens" as such. Open spaces around homes had a functional purpose only: to grow crops, graze animals and maintain flowers that were beneficial for their medicinal properties. Attitudes didn't start changing until the sixteenth century, when the Turks of the Ottoman Empire came along and their pleasure-loving rulers took it upon themselves to add a bit of spice to life.

Big on belly dancing and other lusty pleasures, Turkish sultans also created walled gardens, where they planted tulips—tons of tulips. In fact, they were the first people to cultivate the bulbs. They probably acquired them from adventurers arriving in Constantinople after treks on horseback through Asia. These rough-and-tough guys are believed to have dug up tulips they found growing wild in a windy, lonely region of mountains and high steppes that undulates like a ribbon along the forty degrees line of latitude. (This ribbon passes through what is now the Tien Shan province of China, parts of Turkey,

LOVED LONG AGO: These types of tulips are called 'lily-flowered' because they reminded ancient Turks of lilies.

Iran, Armenia and Azerbaijan. You can still find some species of wild tulips growing there, in dwindling numbers.)

The Turks dubbed their fave new flower *lale*. Within another century, one of their grand viziers, Mehmed, had earned the nickname *Lalizari*, or

CENTURIES OLD: *At the* Hortus Bulborum (or Bulb Garden) *in Limmen, Holland, tulips grown hundreds of years ago are kept in cultivation. Many are too fragile for the mass market.*

lover of tulips. He was so besotted, he had half a million tulips flourishing in his garden, laid out in patterns, like carpets. Hundreds more were wound around archways and obelisks. Portrayed in etchings as a solemn gent in a turban, this potentate also put on elaborate tulip festivals at every new moon, during which nubile young ladies danced naked around huge candlelit vases filled with—what else?—tulips. (The clothed guests were ordered to wear outfits that harmonized with the flowers' colors.)

So great was the passion for tulips among Turkish sultans that they, and their underlings, probably became the first hybridizers of ornamental plants. They constantly tinkered with their collections, developing new tulip varieties. They even imported tulip bulbs from Holland (where the flower started making its mark in the sixteenth century). A register of plants called the *Feranghiz*, maintained during the Ottoman era, listed no fewer than 1,588 tulip types to choose from. In this list—perhaps the world's first plant catalog—the focus was clearly on the sensual qualities of tulips, for each was given a name like 'Lover's Dream,' 'Ruby of Paradise' or 'Beauty's Reward.' The huge selection the Turks had at their disposal is mind-boggling when you

LOVERS TAKE NOTE

Want to "say it with tulips"? Here's what, according to various legends, their colors signify:

Red tulips—declaration of love

Variegated tulips—beautiful eyes

Yellow tulips—hopeless love

Any kind of tulip—fame may be yours

consider that this happened in the eighteenth century, a time when the whole concept of ornamental gardening was in its infancy, and when sophisticated methods of plant hybridization were still a long way off.

Citing the essentials for a "perfect tulip," the Turkish sultans were as precise as any chef writing out a recipe, yet they struck a romantic note, too. In fact, they could have been describing a comely new harem recruit. They listed the flower's vital statistics thus:

> *She has the color of the violet and the curved form of the new moon. Her markings are rightly placed, clean and well-proportioned. Her shape is like the almond, needle-like and ornamented with pleasant rays. Her inner petals are like a well, as they should be; her outer petals are a little open, this too is as it should be. The white ornamental petals are absolutely perfect. She is the chosen of the chosen.*

If this doesn't sound to you like the kind of tulips we know today, you're bang on the mark. What the Turks delighted in *was* an entirely different bulb. Over the centuries, reacting to the whims of public taste, plant hybridizers have bred a whole family of tulips, in many different shapes and sizes—and most modern gardeners would probably turn up their noses at the kind of tulips worshiped back in the heyday of the Ottoman Empire.

The Turkish preference was for *T. acuminata*. It's a spindly-looking specimen, compared with modern, bowl-shaped tulips, and it has odd, pointed petals, in creamy white or red (but often combining both). However, the flower's shape—somewhat like an urn or almond—is very

SPINDLY SPECIMEN:
This funny-looking flower is
T. acuminata. *It was the*
first cultivated tulip. In the
sixteenth century, the citizens
of Constantinople went nuts
over it.

QUITE A CONTRAST:
Over the years, tulips have
gotten bigger. 'Duc van Tol'
(left) was a fave in the 1700s.
Nowadays, we're more likely to
ooh and aah over 'Beauty of
Oxford,' developed in 1961.

distinctive, lending itself well to graphic interpretation. Topped by three stylized petals, this tulip design crops up again and again, in many decorative arts of the Ottoman era, such as tiles, plates and carpets. The Turks also wove the design into their clothing. In New York's Metropolitan

TULIPS TAKE MONET TO NEW HEIGHTS

Impressionist painter Claude Monet's paintings of water lilies were actually inspired by tulips.

Invited to Holland in 1886, the famous French artist (1840–1926) was bowled over by immense red and yellow swaths of tulips, reaching towards the horizon, that confronted him in the bulb fields. "Enough to drive a poor painter crazy—impossible to render with our poor colors," he grumbled.

But try he did. Monet picked up his brushes—and produced five canvases in twelve days. They were bold, luminous works, painted in his (by now) recognizable Impressionistic style. They also set the stage for the final phase of his career.

Monet was particularly impressed by the canals between the bulb fields. Workers piled nipped-off flowers on the edges of these canals, and their brilliant colors were reflected in the water. "On these little canals, we see spots of yellow, like colored rafts in the blue reflection of the sky," he enthused to friends.

The image of flowers floating on a mirror of water became an obsession for Monet, and undoubtedly gave him the idea for the water-lily paintings produced towards the end of his life. He also never forgot those swaths of red and yellow tulips. It was his favorite color combination for flowers, one he duplicated many times, using tulips, at his garden in Giverny, outside Paris.

Museum of Art, there is a sixteenth-century coat of heavy gold brocade, probably once worn by a sultan, that is exquisitely embroidered all over with the unmistakable shape of *T. acuminata*

Some modern gardeners still grow this Turkish delight and say they wouldn't be without it, perhaps due to its curiosity value, for it was the first cultivated tulip. However, *T. acuminata* isn't generally sought-after today. Many bulb suppliers no longer even bother to list it in their catalogs—simply because it comes across as a plain Jane of a flower, a tad on the anorexic side, when contrasted with younger, more nubile members of the tulip family. In fact, it's worth remembering that the blooms of tulips available to us in the twenty-first century are uniformly bigger, plumper and more sensuous than the skimpy versions that inspired the ancient Turks, and others before them, to such heights of passion. So we shouldn't take these beauties for granted.

IMPRESSIONIST INSPIRATION: *The reflections of tulips in bulb field canals fascinated Monet—and led him to create his famous water lily paintings.*

two

The tulip in Europe: Mix-ups, Monkey Business and Plunging Necklines

The tulip is still called *lale* (pronounced *lah-lay*) in Turkey. If it weren't for a goof by a stately gent named Ogier Ghiselin de Busbecq, the rest of the world would probably know it by that name too. We'd be scouring plant catalogs in search of luscious *lales*, not tulips.

The mix-up happened in the sixteenth century, when de Busbecq, a Flemish diplomat, visited Constantinople and misunderstood what an interpreter told him about a new flower he kept

CLASSIC COMEBACK: Out of fashion for years, lily-flowered tulips are popular once again.

seeing. The Turks were fond of wearing this flower, which was red and reminded foreign visitors of a lily, in their turbans. De Busbecq pointed to one, stuck in somebody's headgear, as if to ask its name. The interpreter answered, "*Tolibam.*"

Talk about a case of mistaken identity. Many historians now believe that the interpreter was referring to the turban, not the flower (for "*tolibam,*" which later metamorphosed into "*tulipam,*" meant "turban" in Turkish). Blissfully unaware of the confusion, de Busbecq wrote, once he got home, about the wonderful *tulipam* he had discovered in Turkey—and the name stuck.

Whatever their moniker, these novelty flowers were soon arriving, as bulbs, in the Belgian port of Antwerp. They often came wrapped in bales of cloth from Constantinople. A Dutch botanist friend of de Busbecq, Carolus Clusius, also brought

LEST WE FORGET: At the bulb museum in Limmen, Holland, old tulip varieties aren't allowed to die out.

tulip seeds back and began cultivating them, strictly for scientific purposes, in a botanical garden at Leiden. Unlike de Busbecq, Clusius was a rather snotty fellow: he refused to share the new booty with anybody else. So a few intrepid souls, who recognized the potential of this sensationally pretty flower, scaled the wall of his garden and swiped a few bulbs. In doing so, they instigated a love affair that has lasted over four hundred years.

The sixteenth century Europeans (particularly citizens of the Netherlands) took to the *tulipam* like hummingbirds to hibiscus blooms. For here was a flower that struck them as excitingly different, quite unlike anything they'd ever seen before. The tulip became a status symbol, flaunted by the elite in the same way that expensive cars and Rolex watches are today. As a result, in the beginning years of the seventeenth century, all of Holland became gripped by a frenzy that's now known as "Tulipomania."

Tulipomania could be compared to the Gold Rush of the 1890s or, more recently, the craze to invest in dot.com companies. Many of the people who took part were neither gardeners nor plant fanciers; they simply saw it as a get-rich-quick scheme. As in all such schemes, prices kept escalating based on hearsay, without any relation to the desired object's intrinsic worth. A rumor would start circulating that such and such a person had a monster tulip, ready to dig up and sell in a couple of months, and the bidding wars would start. Big bulbs were the most highly prized, because all tulips were sold by weight. However, no one had any way of knowing just how valuable a particular tulip specimen was going to be, because all the bulbs were traded while they were still growing in the

ONCE HOT: A horticulturist shows off the kind of tulip that the seventeeth century Dutch were wild about.

ground. A specimen that looked promising could prove—once it was removed from the earth—to be far more puny than anyone anticipated.

Once someone acquired the ownership papers to a tulip, he wouldn't necessarily take his purchase home and plant it in his own garden. Often, he'd promptly trade the bulb to somebody else at a higher price, like a short-term trader in the stock market. The men who handled these transactions could pull in as much as 60,000 florins a month (that's $44,000 in today's money, a pretty hefty commission for a broker back in the seventeenth century), and as always, people who could least afford it jumped on the bandwagon.

If they didn't have the cash (and many didn't), starry-eyed Dutch citizens offered their homes or belongings as payment. Magnificent houses on Amsterdam canals were swapped for a single tulip bulb. Tulip merchants wound up on the receiving end of priceless antiques and works of art. One deal cited "a sideboard of ebony decorated with many mirrors and a large painting of flowers." In another, the eager bulb buyer handed over "a new carriage with two dapple-gray horses, a sleigh with horse, a painting of Judas and a painting by Ruysdael"—all for a tulip.

As the mania to acquire tulips spread, country folk got into the act. In the most celebrated case, a farmer traded, for his lone bulb, virtually everything he owned. The list included "two loads of wheat, four loads of rye, four fat oxen, eight fat pigs, twelve sheep, two barrels of butter, a thousand pounds of cheese, two hogsheads of wine, four barrels of special beer, a silver beaker, a suit of clothes and a complete bed, the whole being valued at 2,500 florins." He'd probably have thrown in his wife, if asked. Whether this reckless fellow regretted the deal, or made a mint, isn't known.

At the height of Tulipomania, between 1623 and 1637, the price for one particular tulip, the Semper Augustus, escalated at a rate that resembles modern booms in real estate. In 1624, one Semper Augustus bulb cost 1,200 florins. By the following year the price had leapt to an incredible 3,000 florins. A decade later you'd have had to cough up 10,000 florins to acquire a sample of this striking, and much-admired, red and white striped tulip (the same price as a house on a canal in Amsterdam).

EXPENSIVE EYE CANDY: During Tulipomania, a single bulb of a tulip like this one could cost thousands of dollars.

If you couldn't scrape up enough cash for a bulb, you tried to buy a painting of tulips instead. It seems odd to us today that a simple flower could cost more than a huge oil painting, but that was the reality. Artists were ten a penny in Holland in the seventeenth century, and they cranked out dozens of works to keep up with the demand. What they painted—or

TULIP TEMPTRESS:
Madame de Pompadour,
mistress of Louis XV, decorated
her décolletage with tulips.

SEX AND THE TULIP

Cleavage containing tulips, saucily positioned. That was the fashion during the reign of the Sun King, Louis XIV (1638–1715).

The Dutch weren't the only Europeans to fall head over heels in love with the new flower sensation from Turkey. The French never speculated in tulips, but they nonetheless spent small fortunes on decorating their homes—and their breasts and hair—with the blooms. Florists in Haarlem were kept busy dispatching the flowers to Versailles and other palaces in France. For ladies of the court, it became a status symbol to trim their plunging necklines with the most expensive tulip available. Madame de Pompadour, mistress of Louis XV, loved to decorate her décolletage with tulips.

Some years later, Josephine de Beauharnais, wife of Napoleon Bonaparte, was also entranced drew, or reproduced in etchings—were usually vases of flowers and fanciful garden landscapes, with tulips displayed prominently. These realistically interpreted scenes, full of detail, tend to perplex gardeners nowadays, because they usually show a bunch of blooms that couldn't possibly all be flowering at the same time. However, such paintings weren't intended to

by the flower. It's even believed that Josephine played a hand in the spread of tulips throughout Europe, through her personal connections to a Turkish sultan. According to the story, the exotic Josephine, a creole from Martinique, had an equally enticing cousin. This relative, Aimée de Rivéry, became a concubine in the court of Mahmud II after a bizarre turn of events. (The boat carrying her home to the Caribbean from France got hijacked by Algerian pirates.) Mahmud was enthralled by Aimée's dusky beauty. When she gave birth to a son in 1783, the Turkish ruler held a huge tulip festival to celebrate. His subsequent correspondence with Josephine influenced Franco-Turkish relations. Undoubtedly, the trend to acquire tulips got a boost too.

PRIZED PATTERNS:
This historic tulip, called
'Zilvern,' has the kind of
stripy markings that puzzled
botanists in the seventeenth
century.

POPULAR DESIGN:
Weavers loved the tulip's shape. Here, it's worked into a seventeenth century Austrian embroidery.

be true reflections of nature. Nor were many of them great works of art. People bought one as a showpiece, simply to announce to the world that they too had a piece of the tulip action.

Tulipomania was a bandwagon all right, and efforts were made to stop gullible citizens jumping onto it. Local governments in Holland passed laws against speculation in tulips, but people ignored them. Some artists, usually the ones with genuine talent, took to poking fun at the foolish behavior of the participants in the craze. In a fascinating painting that hangs in the Frans Hals Museum in Haarlem, Hendrik Gerritsoon Pot (1585–1657) depicts a group of people riding in a grand carriage, with tulips sprouting from their heads. He called it *Flora's Wagon of Idiots*. A plump woman—Flora, the tulip goddess—sits triumphantly atop the carriage while her subjects stare ahead with glum expressions, having blown all their money to become members of the "tulip club." Several artists did etchings or caricatures on the same theme. Jan Bruegel II (1601–78) ridiculed tulip traders as greedy monkeys, gobbling rich food and drinking to excess.

These satirical portrayals didn't stop thousands of hitherto sane businessmen, including some leading power-brokers of the day, getting caught up in the mania to trade in tulips. When the crash finally came, in 1637, many people lost everything. A few took poison or drowned themselves in Amsterdam's canals.

The crash was almost as sudden as a modern-day downturn on Wall Street. At a gathering of tulip merchants in 1637, none of them—for some inexplicable reason—received their usual sky-high prices for new bulbs. Whispers spread like wildfire that the market was going soft. People started frantically unloading whatever tulips they had in their possession, at

KALEIDOSCOPE OF COLOR: Hundreds of varieties of tulips are interplanted with other spring-flowering bulbs in Holland's Keukenhof Gardens.

Holland produces three billion tulip bulbs a year. If you placed them in a line, four inches apart, they would circle the equator seven times.
   —**Netherlands Flower Bulb Information Center statistic**

fire sale prices. Within a week or two, things crashed, right to the bottom. Tulip prices never crept back up again (unlike what usually happens in today's stock market), even though some foolhardy buyers hoped they might. The flower's collapse as a financial investment was hardly surprising, since prices were inflated beyond reason—and the whole caper had been absurd in the first place. Economic turmoil followed. The Dutch had, by this time, become big-time travelers and traders; when Tulipomania finally bit the dust, they were buying and selling a variety of goods abroad. Nevertheless, the after-effects of their collective folly over a flower sent shock waves around the world for years.

   Happily, the tulip itself endured. People weren't turned off its charms. The most extraordinary period in their history may have turned into an embarrassing debacle, but the citizens of Holland got back on their feet remarkably quickly. The cultivation of tulips, and of other flowering bulbs, resumed after a few years. Although fortunes could no longer be made from a single bulb, the sensible Dutch developed savvy at marketing tulips en masse—and built themselves a profitable business, selling billions of bulbs to delighted gardeners in many countries.

   Today, tulips are the Netherlands' number-one bulb export. About two billion bulbs are dispatched abroad every year, with over half going to

North America. The Dutch, always very competent farmers, devote nearly 45,000 acres to cultivating flower bulbs, even though they live in a heavily populated country, too flat and close to the sea for comfort, that is only half the size of Maine. While other flower bulbs, like daffodils, hyacinths and alliums, are popular, tulips outstrip their cousins in sales many times over, and they continue to be allocated the lion's share of growing space in the bulb fields.

Holland and the tulip have become as indelibly linked, in the minds of people around the globe, as Camembert cheese and France. When asked what three items conjure up an image of Holland, just about all of us give the same answer: we say "tulips" first, then "windmills," then "wooden shoes." But tulips are always tops—in any language.

THE NEW AND THE OLD: 'Torino' (left) is the kind of tulip that we tend to favor today. It is cup-shaped, with big, showy blooms in plain colors. Back in 1785, however, stripy 'Roi Pepin' was the ideal. People adored patterned, feathered tulips and turned them into garden showpieces.

THEM'S THE BREAKS: THE AFFAIR OF THE APHID

Tulips with bold stripes and jazzy markings aren't particularly admired today; we tend to prefer plain or two-tone colors. In recent years, pastel shades have also become more fashionable than hot hues like red and orange. The opposite was true in the seventeenth century. Stripy, patterned tulips became so sought-after, they contributed to the frenzy of Tulipomania.

Back then, tulips came in one or two colors only. Most were red, yellow or a maroon-purple. But now and then, something extraordinary happened. Stripes and intricate whorls of white would appear, chameleon-like, on the plainly hued tulips, after they came up from the ground in the spring. These mutant markings, which happened rarely, could be strikingly beautiful. On a red tulip they looked rather like streaks of cream, swirled into a bowl of strawberry sauce. Dutch botanists called the markings "breaks," and soon plant experts everywhere were scratching their heads

TA TA TULIPS: In Holland's bulb fields, tulip blooms don't last long. Workers quickly snip them off, so they won't drain strength from the burgeoning bulbs below. Mountains of petals are hauled away on barges bordering the fields.

in exasperation over them. No one could figure out why tulips had the ability to change color like this, seemingly all on their own.

These "broken" tulips were truly unique: no two breaks appeared on a tulip bloom in exactly the same way. They became known as Rembrandt tulips (even though the famous Dutch painter had no connection with the phenomenon himself, and never did paintings of the flowers). Understandably, everyone wanted to get their hands on them. They were the most coveted bulbs, the ones that people swapped their homes and emptied their bank accounts for. However, it proved impossible for anyone to predict when, or where, a break would occur next. Among hundreds of plain tulips planted each fall, by both experienced and amateur growers, only one or two would be decked out, the following spring, with the telltale stripy markings. Desperate to duplicate this effect (and make themselves a bundle of cash) some bulb growers doused their bulb beds in red wine or dye. Others tried chopping bulbs in half and gluing a "broken" tulip to a plain type of tulip. Nothing worked.

The mystery wasn't solved for nearly two centuries. In the 1920s, a meticulous British botanist, Dorothy Cayley, discovered that breaks happened after a certain kind of virus had infected the tulip. This virus was triggered by aphids—minuscule insects, barely visible to the naked eye, that are the bane of gardeners everywhere (for they make a nuisance of themselves on many plants, not just tulips). The tulip changed color as a defense mechanism against the virus. It didn't just decide, on a whim, to deck itself out in a stripy new outfit. Eventually, the virus would kill the bulb.

The British discovery came far too late for the hapless Dutch who first experienced the amazing side-effects of aphids. Sadly, all those people who lusted after "broken" tulips, selling everything they owned to acquire them, never did figure out what was going on. But them's the breaks in the tangled tale of the tulip.

three

The Tulip in North America: Presidents, Parades and a Queen's Gift

It's fitting that the most famous song about tulips was penned by an American, Cole Porter. That's because an incredible number of Americans take a regular "tiptoe through the tulips." Nearly one billion tulip bulbs are exported to the United States from the Netherlands every year (U.S. growers raise 250,000 more), and the bulk of

MELLOW YELLOW: This shade of tulip is becoming popular again, after being shunted aside for a couple of decades.

PREFERRED BY THE PREZ; Thomas Jefferson, the third U.S. president, loved flamboyant tulips like this 'Flaming Parrot.'

them are bought by home gardeners. Other flowering bulbs, like daffodils and crocus, don't even come close in terms of sales.

When they get down on their hands and knees each fall to plant tulips, these gardeners (and millions more in Canada) are participating in a rite that has been observed virtually since the New World was colonized. The tulip, originally from Turkey, has now become as American as apple pie. Asked to name a flowering bulb, nearly 80 percent of U.S. citizens, irrespective of where they live, immediately say "the tulip." Even those who profess to know nothing about plants can describe how it looks.

Peter Stuyvesant would have been pleased with this turn of events. Born in the Netherlands, Stuyvesant (1592–1672) was a celebrated governor of

New York (then known as Nieuw Amsterdam) and one of the first people to grow tulips in North America. This colonial administrator liked the spring-blooming flowers so much that he brought some bulbs across the Atlantic, tucked into his luggage, and planted them in the garden surrounding the governor's mansion. Other famous figures in history followed suit. George Washington (1732–1799) wrote meticulous notes in his journals about the tulips at his plantation in Mount Vernon, Virginia.

TULIP TOUTER: New York governor Peter Stuyvesant was one of the first people to plant tulips in North America.

REMINDERS OF HOME: In colonial Williamsburg, Virginia, tulips provided settlers with a comforting link to the Old World.

Not long afterwards, the third U.S. president, Thomas Jefferson (1743–1826), was doing the same thing. The author of several gardening books, Jefferson couldn't bear to be parted from his beloved tulips (and other spring-flowering bulbs) at the family estate in Monticello, Virginia. He wrote letters to his granddaughter, Ann Cary Randolph, praising these "belles of the day [that] have their short reign of beauty and splendor and retire." When traveling in Europe, he eagerly sought out new varieties of tulips and had them sent home for his gardeners to plant. Jefferson clearly had a taste for the flamboyant: he favored double-flowered varieties, plus

THE TULIP AS TALISMAN

Everyone, young and old, likes tulips. That makes them a handy aid for charitable organizations, community groups and schools. The Parkinson's Foundation raises tens of thousands of dollars every fall from sales of tulips. They are also used to raise money for programs battling drug use.

In one neighborhood of Toronto, tulips honor local men and women who served overseas during the two world wars. Every year, the Swansea Horticultural Society plants 150 'Legion Brilliant' tulips for the ones who came home. Twenty-two more tulips, of a variety called 'Legion Gold,' are put in beside them, to commemorate those who died.

FUNDRAISER: 'Engadin,' a greigii tulip, is popular with charities such as the Parkinson's Foundation.

parrot tulips, in red, green and yellow. He also made a beeline for the *baguets*, the most fashionable (and expensive) tulips of the late seventeenth and early eighteenth century. They had huge cup-shaped blooms, capable, it was said, of "holding a pint of wine." (*Baguets* have since disappeared from bulb catalogs because they are considered too tender for cultivation in gardens.)

What undoubtedly appealed to these famous figures—and to ordinary colonial settlers who contributed to the tulip craze—was not just the beauty of the blooms, but the sense of order they bestowed. For in those days, the countryside surrounding populated areas of the U.S. and Canada was considered a hostile and threatening place. People sought to tame nature, not to invite it in willy-nilly, and tulips, imported from Europe, were a reassuring presence. In colonial towns like Williamsburg, Virginia, they became a fixture in flower beds. Graced with tall, straight stems, sculptured blooms and a formal air, tulips fitted in perfectly with the ideal of what a "civilized" garden should look like.

FORMAL ROWS: *This style of growing tulips, shown at Williamsburg, Virginia, fit the colonial ideal of a 'civilized' garden.*

This idea, that the landscape needed to be brought under control, with a firm hand, persisted for centuries. It ultimately led to the uniformity of immaculate, trimmed lawns around every North American home, and to the

WAVES OF COLOR: Tulips strut in a public park in Ottawa. This regimented style of planting, popular in the 1960s, is now going out of fashion.

rigid, all-in-a-row style of planting tulips that was so popular in public parks as late as the 1980s. In the past decade, however, attitudes have started to shift. Perhaps because our cities are now perceived to be more dangerous than the countryside, a "natural" environment is what everyone hankers after. Vast expanses of trimmed turf are no longer fashionable. Indeed, you can't open a gardening magazine nowadays without reading stories that proclaim, with the self-righteousness of an evangelist, that Joe and Mary So-and-So have "got rid of their lawn."

As part of this trend, tulips have shrugged off their stays too. In both public landscaping schemes and home gardens, people now tend to plant these spring-flowering bulbs in a freer style, grouping them together in clumps or cascading

CLOSE TOGETHER: *Modern gardeners prefer to grow tulips in tight groups, rather than rows. Here, they're interspersed with* muscari *and azaleas.*

drifts. No one gives a hoot if their stems arch and bend, or if the flower heads look a bit "blowsy." Those lines of red soldier tulips that used to be seen everywhere are marching off into oblivion.

While planting styles continue to evolve, one thing remains unchanged: our insatiable appetite for this flowering bulb. The tulip could, in fact, be called "the forever flower," for its popularity has remained undiminished for centuries, and the tulip shows no signs of being reduced to a minor role in the garden of the new millennium. Every year, bulb catalogs are sent out, bursting with pictures of tulips. They list tantalizing new varieties here, old faves there—and millions of us buy a bunch, eager to put them in the ground. Planting tulips is an end-of-summer ritual that most gardeners indulge in as a matter of course (provided we live in the kind of climate where tulips can grow). It wouldn't occur to us to skip it, because come spring, no one wants to miss out on the time-honored tradition of, as Cole Porter so aptly put it, taking a "tiptoe through the tulips."

Where to see tulips

Tulips in the tens of thousands. They burst into bloom across North America every spring, in public parks and at tulip festivals. So great is the

FEAST FOR THE EYES: Tulips burst forth in public parks around the world every spring. Here, in Holland's Keukenhof Gardens, they're mixed with fritillaria imperialis *(right) and late-blooming* narcissus. *The tree in the background is a magnolia.*

> The tulips should be behind bars like dangerous animals
> They are opening like the mouth of some great African cat
> —Sylvia Plath, "Tulips"

ascendancy of the tulip that at least a dozen of these festivals have sprung up, mostly in towns and cities where Dutch immigrants settled.

Holland, Michigan, claims the distinction of having paid homage to tulips longer than anywhere else. Back in 1929, a biology teacher, Lida Rogers, suggested adopting the tulip as the town's emblem, and her idea led to the Tulip Time Festival. Lasting for ten days in mid-May, this huge extravaganza now features floats, parades and dancers clacking around in clogs, and it draws more than a million visitors. Sometimes, even U.S. presidents drop by.

Pella, Iowa, the birthplace of Wyatt Earp, kicks off its cowboy boots to honor another local luminary—Dutchman Hendrik Scholte, who founded the town—at its Tulip Festival each May. Citizens plant over 60,000 tulip bulbs, imported from Holland. Other mass plantings are featured at festivals in many locations, including Orange City, Iowa; Albany, New York; and Truro, Nova Scotia.

In the temperate climate of Washington's Skagit Valley and the Willamette Valley of Oregon, the tulip struts its stuff a bit earlier, in April. More than a million visitors head to tulip festivals in these states. Besides

STATE STAR: 'Mount Tacoma' celebrates Washington State, where many spring bulbs are now grown. Tulip festivals are held there every April.

drinking in displays of flowers, they can tour bulb fields and see how the most popular flowering bulb gets its start in life.

A Queen says thanks—with tulips

The largest tulip festival in the world, often featuring five million flowers, takes place in Ottawa. It came about because Queen Juliana of the Netherlands wanted to show how grateful she was to the Canadian people.

Forced to flee to Canada during World War II, the Dutch royal family waited out the Nazi occupation of their homeland in Ottawa. (The Queen's youngest daughter was born there.) In 1946, as a thank-you gift, Queen Juliana dispatched 100,000 tulip bulbs to the city—the first installment of a perpetual bequest that has continued ever since.

Each fall, the Dutch royals (and the country's exporters and growers) provide Ottawa with 20,000 free tulip bulbs. Planted around the Parliament Buildings and in public parks, these form the basis of the two-week-long festival, held in mid-May. It has grown so large that Ottawa is now recognized as the Tulip Capital of North America.

In 2002, Ottawa's Tulip Festival celebrates its fiftieth birthday. Gardeners all over the city will take part in the anniversary by planting fifty tulips each in their front yards.

PICTURE POSTCARD: *Ottawa's Parliament Buildings are surrounded by a blaze of color every spring, as millions of tulips burst into bloom. The city hosts the largest tulip festival in North America, drawing visitors from around the world.*

four

𝒜 Tiptoe Through Tulip Varieties: Parrots, Watermelons and the Name Game

Just about everybody knows what tulips look like. They have long, straight stems, pointed green leaves and big, cup-shaped flowers, which sit on top of the stems. Right?

Well, yes—and no. While many tulips do fit the above description, the standard, cup-shaped

NOT YOUR TYPICAL TULIP: Frothy confections like 'Blue Parrot' provoke mixed reactions. Some gardeners love their scalloped petals and brilliant colors. To others, they're "too gaudy."

FIT FOR A PARADE:
'Olympic Flame' is a Darwin
hybrid tulip.

type of flower is only part of the picture. That's because the world of the tulip is surprisingly large and complex. Those "typical" tulips that we see everywhere, planted en masse in public parks, belong to a big, extended family, a family in which every relative is blessed with its own distinct appearance and attributes. Some types of tulips are shaped like classical urns. A few resemble roses or peonies, with many layers of petals. Others may be as frilly and flamboyant as a can-can dancer's skirt. At least one tulip is slender as a fashion model, with petals that are pointed, instead of being rounded and voluptuous. You can also find some that have such small, inconspicuous flowers, they don't even look like tulips.

Tulip heights vary too. Although they are often planted to resemble soldiers on a parade ground—all about a foot tall and boringly lined up in rows—tulips are sometimes so long and leggy, they will flop crazily over other flowers in the garden. At the other end of the spectrum you find stubby little tulips, only a few inches high—and several specimens that sprawl, octopus-like, along the ground, with star-shaped flowers popping up from their trailing foliage.

All told, there are about fifteen different classifications of tulips. These classes are themselves subdivided into hundreds of different colors, or

TOUGH LITTLE NUMBERS: Species tulips like Fosteriana 'Purissima' cope better with difficult growing conditions than their hybrid cousins.

combinations of colors. It's a confusing collection, all right, but there are some pointers through this botanical maze. The class that a tulip belongs to is always listed first, then its variety comes afterwards, in single quotes. For example: a Darwin 'Clara Butt' means it's a Darwin class of tulip, with 'Clara Butt' denoting its color or variety (in this case, pink). When you add up all the classes and varieties, they constitute a truly amazing figure: over 2,600 different kinds of tulips currently growing in countries around the world. What's even more remarkable is that every one of them, large or small, is descended from those "primitive" tulips found growing in the wilds of Asia Minor centuries ago.

Which is best? Take your pick. Tulips, like all flowers, are strictly a matter of personal taste. However, when thumbing through a bulb catalog, wondering which to buy, it's helpful to remember that all tulips, whatever their appearance, belong to one of three categories. They are *early-flowering*, *mid-season-flowering* or *late-flowering*—occasionally all three.

How you define these categories depends upon where you live. *Early-flowering* can mean as early as March in some areas of the U.S. and in western Canada, or as late as May in northern U.S. states and eastern Canadian provinces. *Mid-season-flowering* tulips generally begin blooming about three weeks after their early-blooming cousins. *Late-flowering* varieties start strutting their stuff about two weeks after that (although local climate fluctuations will often skew the timing). Smart gardeners plant tulips from all three categories, so they have varieties in bloom throughout the spring season.

A description of the different types of tulips follows.

Single early tulips

Consistently popular—and instantly recognizable—they have cup-shaped blooms, with petals that are rounded at the tip. Among the first to bloom, these tulips have sturdy stems that are usually from 14″ to 18″ (36–46 cm) long. The group includes 'Apricot Beauty,' a gentle blend of pale pink and apricot; 'Christmas Dream,' which is cherry pink (despite the name, it won't bloom as early as Christmas unless you force it in a pot, indoors); 'Generaal de Wet,' an old variety that's bright orange and named after a bigwig from the South African Boer War; and 'Keizerkroon,' another oldie, developed way back in 1750, which is decked out in jazzy red and yellow stripes.

OLD FAITHFUL: 'Keizerkroon,' first developed in 1750, is still a big seller.

Single late tulips

These have longer stems (from 22″ to 28″/55–70 cm) than their early-blooming

FLORISTS' FAVE: 'Sorbet' has big, showy blooms and looks good in vases with other flowers.

cousins. The flowers are big and showy, so they're a good choice for floral arrangements. They come in a rainbow of colors, including: 'Asta Nielsen,' a sulfur yellow; 'Cordell Hull,' which is creamy white and flamed with bright red; 'Menton,' whose rose petals are edged with peach; and 'Queen of Night,' probably the darkest tulip of all, with big velvety petals that are maroon-black.

Double tulips

With their many layers of petals, these look a bit like peonies. Doubles bloom early, mid-season and late—and they often last longer in the garden than single tulips. They need a sheltered location, as their blooms can be top-heavy. The group includes: 'Angélique,' a perennially popular variety in gentle hues of pink; 'Clara Carder,' purple with a white base; and 'Monte Carlo,' buttercup yellow tinted with red, which is particularly long-lasting.

LIKE A PEONY: Double tulips such as 'Clara Carder' are a novelty and they last a long time.

NO BUGS HERE: *A Dutch bulb inspector checks stocks. Many diseases and insects can attack tulips, but the industry is vigilant.*

HOW TULIPS GET THEIR NAMES

What do Shakespeare, Einstein, Barbra Streisand and astronaut Neil Armstrong have in common? They all have a tulip named after them.

So do some cities—like Leningrad, New York, Toronto and Pasadena. Place names of other sorts figure prominently too: you can find tulips called 'Mount Everest' and 'Empire State Building.' Then there are storybook characters, such as 'Pinocchio' and 'Mickey Mouse.'

Tulips wind up with their colorful—and sometimes puzzling—names in a couple of ways. Bulb growers may decide that a person, place, thing or event has a special meaning for them, and will baptize a new tulip accordingly. Or requests may be sent to the International Flower Bulb Center in Holland, asking growers to name an upcoming addition to the tulip roster after some-one or something in a certain country. Some requests come via embassies, on behalf of governments, while others originate with private individuals. Whatever their source, being immortalized in the form of a tulip is an honor accorded to only a few.

Whoever or whatever receives this honor, virtually every new tulip vari-ety is developed in the same way. All of them start out in Holland, where private growers use a painstaking process called hybridizing. This involves mixing together the pollen from two different parent tulips—each with desirable elements of form, color and fragrance—to produce a different flower. Sometimes this cross-breeding has marvelous results; more often, it doesn't. New tulip hybrids are never overnight sensations. Even if a crossing is successful, it takes five years to grow a new tulip bulb from seed, and many more years to get that bulb into production.

Darwin tulips

Named after the naturalist Charles Darwin, these are probably the world's most-planted tulips. Sturdy and dependable in cool and wet regions (although they do not perform well in California), they have familiar cup-shaped flowers, and were developed not by the Dutch but by an amateur French grower, M.J. Lenglart, in the nineteenth century. Probably the toughest tulip of them all—the classic 'Apeldoorn,' which is bright red—belongs to this group. There's also 'Golden Apeldoorn,' which is equally tenacious in the garden. Once planted, both varieties will keep popping up, spring after spring.

BOLD AND BEAUTIFUL: Darwin hybrid tulips like 'Striped Oxford' have big, luscious blooms and knockout designs on their petals.

Other varieties include: 'Elizabeth Arden,' which has salmon-pink petals striped with a deeper pinkish violet; 'Tender Beauty,' which has a rose-red flower head edged with ivory white; 'Konigin Wilhelmina,' scarlet etched with orange; and 'Orange Goblet,' a huge tulip that is fiery orange with a yellow base.

Also part of the Darwin class are some varieties of Rembrandt-like tulips. These have been bred by modern hybridizers to look like the celebrated "broken" tulips that drove the Dutch crazy in the sixteenth century. They are single-colored tulips whose petals are "flamed," or striped with a contrasting color.

LIKE HER LIPSTICK: Hybrid 'Elizabeth Arden,' a Darwin, is salmon pink, flushed with light violet.

THE IMPOSSIBLE DREAM

Black tulips. Everyone wants them. No one—so far—can supply them.

Way back in 1593, plant hybridizers at the University of Leiden began trying to come up with a tulip that was truly black. A quarter of a century later, they were still trying. French author Alexandre Dumas wrote about their elusive quest in *The Black Tulip*. Full of intrigue and absurdities (his protagonists doused their tulip bulbs in black dye and stored them in a dark room), the novel was an instant best-seller in Paris in 1850.

Today, we're closer. You can find several so-called "black" tulips, but in reality they're all a deep purple or reddish brown, because the chemical composition of pure black is impossible to achieve in a flower. 'Queen of Night,' developed in 1944, comes the closest. A late bloomer, it has big, sensuous flowers that

CLOSE, BUT NOT QUITE: 'Black Parrot' is one of several so-called "black" tulips. In reality, they're all deep purple or reddish brown.

are the color—and texture—of deep maroon velvet. Other "black" tulips include: 'Burgundy,' a lily-flowered variety, which is a deep purplish violet; 'Black Parrot,' a frilly, flamboyant offering whose petals are deep purple on the outside, but blacker on the inside; and 'Black Diamond,' a single late-flowering variety that's a dark reddish brown, with burnt umber edges and a deep purple interior.

Black is forever beautiful where tulips are concerned. 'Queen of Night' is consistently one of the biggest sellers around the world.

Triumph tulips

A big group, developed by crossing single early tulips with later-flowering ones. They bloom early and mid-season, and closely resemble the Darwins. They got their name because, back in 1933, Dutch hybridizers considered it a triumph to have bred such showy yet practical specimens. With their sturdy stems, Triumph tulips cope well in cold

STURDY STEMS: Triumph tulip 'Mexico' is practical and pretty. It copes well with cold, wind and rain.

weather, wind and rain. They grow prolifically in public parks and gardens. Varieties include: 'Bing Crosby,' a glowing scarlet; 'New Design,' whose creamy petals turn pink as the flower matures; 'Mexico,' a cherry red; 'Negrita,' a new variety with rich purple flowers frosted in silver; and 'Helmar,' a sporty primrose-yellow-and-burgundy combination that's unusually tall 22"/55 cm).

Lily-flowered tulips

Highly fashionable nowadays, these graceful tulips were also favorites of Turkish sultans. Mid-season bloomers, they have long stems with flower heads shaped like classical Greek urns. They are called lily-flowered because to early Dutch botanists, they looked like lilies. 'White Triumphator,' which has pure white petals, is particularly sought-after by modern gardeners because it looks fantastic with other flowers. (Despite the misleading name, it's not a Triumph tulip.) Other varieties include: 'China Pink,' whose satin pink petals fade to white at the base; and 'West Point,' whose petals, in primrose yellow, are sharply pointed.

MAKING A POINT: Lily-flowered 'West Point' has sharply-defined petals that stand out in the garden.

Parrot tulips

Gardeners either love these tulips or hate them. That's because they are unquestionably the Las Vegas showgirls of the springtime garden, with long, swaying stems topped by frilly, brilliantly colored flowers—which do indeed resemble the ruffle on a parrot's head. Too striking for some, they are nonetheless one of the "hottest" tulips to plant these days.

HOT STUFF: Parrot tulips often look as flashy as Las Vegas showgirls.

Among them: 'Flaming Parrot,' the tallest of the group (it reaches 28"/70 cm while other varieties are 20"/50 cm), with chrome yellow petals ignited by red; 'Estella Rijnveld,' which looks like raspberry ripple ice cream; 'Orange

ONE OF THE TALLEST: 'Flamingo Parrot' grows to a formidable 28"/70 cm.

Favorite,' a zingy combination of bright orange and pink streaked with green; 'White Parrot,' its pure white blooms as ruffled as a carnation; 'Black Parrot,' glossy and black, with fluted petals; and 'Professor Röntgen,' which is a veritable riot of lemon, green, chrome and orange-red.

Fringed tulips

Similar to parrot tulips but not as widely grown, their petals are cut and spiky at the edges, like the fringe on a shawl. This gives the pale vari-

UNUSUAL: The edges of fringed tulips look like lace. This one is a double variety called 'Fringed Beauty.'

eties a decidedly lacy look in the garden. They include: 'Canova,' which is purple with a white fringe; 'Fancy Frills,' a concoction of pink and white stripes; and a very tall variety, 'Maja' (26"/65 cm), which is light yellow.

Viridiflora tulips

These are instantly recognizable by a green streak running through the center of each exterior petal. In some varieties, the flower heads are green all over until they open. (*Viridiflora* means "green-flowered" in Latin.) Like the parrots and fringed tulips, these are often either adored or detested. Some gardeners feel that green looks all wrong on a tulip flower; to others it's an eye-catching novelty. Their heights vary, as do the shape of their petals. One popular variety in North America is 'Greenland' (also called 'Groenland'), which is bright pink combined with green. It's often called the watermelon tulip. Others include: 'Artist,' which is mostly a rose-apricot color and has exotic twisted petals; 'Hummingbird,' which mixes golden yellow with green; and a new variety, 'Spring Green,' which grows 20"/50 cm tall and changes color—from pale green to mostly white—as the flowers develop.

CONTROVERSIAL: *The green streak that runs through Viridiflora tulips is loved by some gardeners. Others think it looks odd.*

Species tulips

A big, confusing group, some of which don't even look like "regular" tulips. Among them are the following.

T. batalinii: Considered by many to be fragrant and worthy of more recognition, it grows about 4″ to 6″ (10–15 cm) tall and puts out lots of small, plump flowers in soft yellow for more than a month, starting mid-spring. It also comes in other colors: 'Apricot Jewel,' 'Yellow Jewel,' 'Red Gem' and 'Bronze Charm.'

NOT WIDELY KNOWN: Prolific bloomer T. batalinii *is just starting to be discovered by gardeners.*

T. clusiana: Nicknamed the "lady tulip" for its dainty, pointy petals, this mid-season bloomer was a favorite of British gardening icon Vita Sackville-West. It's named after Carolus Clusius, the Dutch botanist who was instrumental in bringing tulips to Europe. A two-tone tulip, it looks striped, because its interior petals are white while the outer ones are rose-pink. It grows about 10″/25 cm high.

DAINTY DELIGHT: British gardening icon Vita Sackville-West called T. Clusiana *"the lady tulip."*

DEMYSTIFYING SPECIES TULIPS

A lot of people are puzzled by the word "species," especially when it's applied to tulips. This is hardly surprising. Generally speaking, species is the umbrella term used to describe families of plants—*any* plants. What, then, are "species tulips"? How do they differ from other tulips?

In a nutshell, species refers to tulip varieties that are closest cousins to the original wild tulips found growing in Asia. Most are smaller, tougher and less showy than their "citified" relatives, the hybrid tulips. Hybrids are the most popular, and widely planted, kind of tulips. They are classed into categories like Triumph, Darwin, Lily-flowered and Parrot, and they have been bred by bulb growers to produce big, luscious flowers.

However, species tulips are growing in popularity with many gardeners because, while their flowers tend to be small, they adapt well to difficult conditions, like poor soil or cold winters. Most also have a longer blooming period than hybrids, and they multiply easily in the garden. While they have a "wild" ancestry, the species tulips we buy today are all bred by growers in Holland. Although you can still find species tulips growing wild in some countries, it is illegal to dig them up—or to pick their flowers.

"Species tulips are perfect bulbs for harsh, continental climates," writes Lauren Springer, Denver-based author of *The Undaunted Garden*.

ON THE WILD SIDE: Species tulips like this T. fosteriana *'Juan' are the closest relatives of the original wild tulips found growing in Asia. But all tulips are now bred by Dutch growers.*

DIFFERENT DIMENSIONS:
T. fosteriana *has oblong flowers which open wider than many other tulips.*

MIXED REACTIONS: Gardeners love or detest the mottled leaves of T. greigii. *This one's called 'Gratia.'*

T. fosteriana: There are several different types of this early-blooming tulip. Most are instantly recognizable by their gray-green mottled leaves and oblong flowers, which are longer (and open wider) than other species tulips. They also often have brilliant colors and broad leaves. Varieties include: 'Candela,' which is lemon yellow; 'Easter Parade,' bright red and yellow; and 'Princeps,' bright red with a bronzy green base.

T. greigii: A very "different-looking" tulip, with short stems and striking foliage. Gardeners tend to love it or hate it, because the leaves are surprisingly large and wide, and mottled with reddish-brown stripes. This toughie blooms early to mid-season and has pointy blooms a bit like its lily-flowered cousins. They usually come in red, yellow or white, or in combinations of these colors. Varieties include: popular 'Cape Cod,' which is apricot edged with yellow; 'Pinocchio,' a scarlet and white combination; 'Yellow Dawn,' rose pink with a wide yellow band; and single-colored 'Red Riding Hood,' which is a brilliant red.

T. kaufmanniana: The first tulip to flower in spring, it was discovered growing wild in Turkestan in the 1850s by August van Regel, curator of the Imperial Botanic Gardens in St. Petersburg, and it has been a fave with many gardeners ever since. Low-growing, it's often called the "water-lily tulip" because its petals open wide in the sun—and then close up to a cone shape in the evening. Varieties include: 'Stresa,' which is yellow with large red triangles on its petals; 'Glück,' carmine red edged with yellow, which has interesting leaves striped with chocolate; and 'Shakespeare,' a blend of orange and apricot on the outside with an interior of salmon shot through with red.

LIKE A LILY: Popular T. kaufmanniana *varieties like 'Racine' are known as "water-lily tulips" because their petals open wide.*

T. praestans: Sometimes found wild in the Provence region of France, this tulip is short and (usually) brick red, although there are some other varieties. Appearing early in the season, it often has four flower heads bursting from one stem.

POPS UP IN PROVENCE: T. praestans *is sometimes found growing wild in southern France.*

Sweet Smelling: Charming T. sylvestris *is small but fragrant. It also lasts a long time.*

T. sylvestris: A sweetly scented novelty tulip, it is popular with gardeners because it blooms for a long time. It has long, nodding, golden yellow flowers on stems that grow about 10″/25 cm high. Curiously, the flowers open sideways, in the shape of a six-pointed star. They can be found growing wild in southern Italy and Sardinia, and are extremely tough when planted in a garden.

T. tarda: The word tarda means "late" in Latin, but this (the tiniest of all tulips, at 4″/10 cm high) is one worth waiting for. Discovered way back in the 1590s in Turkestan (and unchanged in appearance since then), it sends up leaves that sprawl along the ground, plus plenty of chrome yellow flowers edged in stark white. As many as six star-shaped flowers will appear on one stem.

Worth the Wait: Late bloomer T. tarda *sprawls along the ground and is great in a rock garden.*

T. Turkestanica: This little gem sports creamy white flowers, shaped like stars, that have a yellow blotch in the center. It is one of the first tulips to appear after the winter. Gardeners praise its prolific growth habit: as many as nine flowers are produced on each of the 8″/20 cm stems.

EARLY BIRD: one of the first tulips to appear in spring, T. Turkestanica *has lots of flowers.*

T. urumiensis: A low-growing, meandering variety, it puts out a rosette of leaves from which short stems, bearing starlike flowers, burst forth. The petals are golden yellow with an attractive dark green band running through them, on the outside. It flowers early in the season.

BLOOMS LIKE STARS: T. urumensis *is a rambler that grows only a few inches high, with blooms aplenty.*

TOUGH TO DEVELOP: Dutch growers have mixed results with multi-flowered tulips like 'Georgette.' They have big flower heads, all sprouting from one stem.

Multiflora tulips

These are comparatively new—and uncommon—in the tulip world. Unlike other hybrids, they have several big flower heads growing on each stem. They were developed by Dutch growers who crossed several varieties of species tulips, and they grow about 20"/50 cm tall. Because they are still in the development stages, there are few varieties, and they are not widely available. Some multifloras that have been successfully introduced into the bulb market include: 'Happy Family,' a Triumph multi-flowering tulip with two-toned pink flowers; and 'Georgette,' a single late-flowering variety whose yellow flowers are tipped with red.

TULIPS THAT SMELL NICE

The majority of tulips have no real scent. However, some people find that tulips develop a pleasing fragrance after being cut and brought indoors. As well, there are a few varieties with a definite perfume. In the scent stakes, Dutch bulb growers say these three stand out:

• 'Angélique': A gorgeous tulip that's pale pink with double blooms, like a peony. Blooms late. Smell is similar to some roses.

• 'Apricot Beauty': A perennial favorite, with pale pinkish-orange blooms delicately streaked with red. Blooms early—and is good for forcing indoors. Perfume is sweet and piquant, like honey and cloves mixed together.

• 'Prinses Irene': Orange, with a purple flash on the outer petals. Mid-season bloomer. Fresh scent that some say is like lemon tea sweetened with honey.

SNIFFABLE: *Multi-petaled 'Angelique' is one of the few fragrant tulips. It smells a lot like roses.*

TULIPS THAT LAST

Garden writers often describe tulips as "one-hit wonders." That is, they bloom for one season, then do a disappearing act.

Unfortunately, it's true. Many tulip varieties—too many—bloom spectacularly for one spring but never come up again. This is particularly true of big, luscious hybrid tulips. Babied by Dutch growers under optimum conditions, these classes of tulips—so tempting in bulb catalogs—are far more finicky than their smaller, uncosseted cousins, the species tulips.

How long any tulip lasts in the garden depends a lot on the climate and location where it is grown. Because they first flourished in the dry, cold, sandy mountains of Asia, that's what tulips, whatever their type, still prefer. If these bulbs could talk, they would say: "Give us cold winters with snow cover, a good baking in summertime, a flower bed that slopes a bit—and excellent sandy loam that drains well. Please!"

According to one bulb expert, Dugald Cameron, even when these requirements are met, hybrid tulips will come up in the garden for a maximum of three or four seasons. However, planted in the kind of average soil that most gardeners are stuck with, most last no more than two seasons—

PLAIN BUT PROLIFIC:
Tough as nails 'Apeldoorn' will keep coming up in the garden, year after year.

and often it's only one. You get one stunning display in spring, and that's it. Ta-ta tulips.

Species tulips are another matter altogether. Many varieties are so durable, they often become permanent fixtures in the garden. In a location that suits them, they multiply easily and will keep appearing, as regularly as clockwork, every spring. Some varieties that adapt particularly well to the climate in some parts of the northern U.S. and southern Canada are: *T. tarda*, *T. kaufmanniana*, *T. greigii*, *T. fosteriana*, *T. sylvestris* and *T. armena*.

The process of getting tulips to keep coming back in the garden is called naturalizing. While most hybrid tulips refuse to naturalize, a few will, if the conditions are right. The best ones to try are the Darwins, and in particular, two classic varieties: 'Apeldoorn' (red) and 'Golden Apeldoorn' (canary yellow). Lily-flowered tulips also have staying power in some areas of North America. Many gardeners have success with: 'White Triumphator'; yellow 'West Point'; 'Ballade,' which is mauve with white edging; and 'Mariette,' a rose pink variety that multiplies particularly well.

DOESN'T DISAPPEAR: Some gardeners find that lily-flowered 'Mariette' multiplies well in the garden.

five

$\mathcal{T}$ulips 101: Everything You Need to Know About Growing Them

The trendy world of tulips

There's something about tulips that captivates most of us, even if we aren't gardeners. Perhaps it's their kaleidoscope of colors: they can be as loud and strident as a rock band, or as softly sensuous as a piece of pale silk. Or maybe their simple, sculptured shape holds the key to their allure—for every curvaceous bloom always seems

COLORS THAT CAPTIVATE: *The sight of a swath of tulips in springtime enchants most people. These are 'Red Emperor' species tulips* T. fosteriana.

ELEGANT APPEAL: Lily-flowered tulips, shaped like classical urns, have come back into vogue.

so amazingly perfect as it unfolds from a tight green bud. Or it could be the way those buds nudge up from the ground, like green fingernails, every spring, making us feel instantly uplifted after the long, gray months. Then there's the magical look that tulips have when they are massed together, all blooming at the same time. Their great sweeps of color, waving in the wind, are a reminder of just how glorious—and fleeting—the manifestations of nature can be.

Whatever the reason, tulips have universal appeal, and they are a fixture, every spring, in dozens of countries. An inevitable consequence of their familiarity is that they—like anything else that keeps coming and going with the seasons—are subject to the whims of fashion. In fact, the world has always followed styles in tulips in somewhat the same way that teenage girls nowadays copy the lengths of skirts worn by pop stars.

Back in the fifteenth century, Turkish sultans favored masses of tulips crammed into their walled gardens, and they liked the lily-flowered kind, shaped like classical urns. Yet a hundred years later, in Holland, the fashion had switched to acquiring one lone tulip, boldly striped in yellow or red and planted in splendid isolation (undoubtedly because, in those days of Tulipomania, it was so difficult and expensive for the Dutch to obtain any tulips at all). Preferably bowl-shaped with lots of feathery petals, this single tulip became the focal point in the garden, and every-thing else—hedges, pathways, other flowers, ornaments—was strategically placed to emphasize it.

WHAT IS A TULIP?

Unlike most garden plants, which develop strictly from roots and stems, tulips are spring-flowering bulbs. Round and fleshy, bulbs are covered in many layers of skin, like an onion. They are planted several inches below the soil surface, from whence they send forth roots, stems, leaves and flowers.

All bulbs are, in essence, buds hidden in the earth. Their "skins," called tunics, are white, fleshy scales. These contain food reserves to feed the embryonic flowers inside the bulb. After being planted in the fall, the flat underside of each bulb—called the basal plate—sends out roots, then flowers and new leaves start to develop deep inside, fed and protected by their scaly overcoat.

In springtime, leaves and stems, topped by flower buds, emerge from this center. Once flowering has finished, the bulb sloughs off this

ONION-LIKE: *Every tulip bulb is covered in many layers of skin, called tunics.*

HEAT WANTED: If it's cold and rainy all summer, luscious blooms like these lily-flowered 'Ballade' may not have a chance to develop properly.

season's scales, rather like a snake discarding its dried-up skin—then it gets busy developing a brand new overcoat. Above-ground, bulb foliage may dry up and look "dead," but down below a food storage unit has swung into operation. Fleshy layers of scales start building up on the bulb, and another flower embryo begins to form at the center. Often tiny bulblets, called "maidens" or offsets, will develop too, attached to the bottom of bulb.

Ideally, the weather must be fairly warm during the day (68–75°F/20–24°C), dropping to 60°F/16°C at night, for this process to happen effectively. It should also be dry. That's because the first wild tulips, which grew in Asia, started developing onion-like layers, to store food, as a protective measure against heat and drought in that part of the world. Modern tulips have been bred to be more adaptable (because they must grow in all kinds of climates), but they still go through the same basic life cycle. If the summer is very rainy and cool, the end result, the following spring, may be fewer tulips popping up in the flower bed, because the bulbs didn't receive the "trigger" to build up those new layers of scales properly.

Today, most of us don't have walled gardens—nor do we pay fortunes for a single tulip. Yet nothing has really changed. Tulip styles still come and go, according to public flights of fancy. A certain color will be highly desirable for a few years, then another shade is suddenly the "in" thing and everyone wants to get their hands on it. The same is true of tulip shapes and planting styles. The fact is, people have never

PLAIN ONES ONLY, PLEASE: These kinds of tulip colors have been in vogue for years, but now gardeners are starting to turn to jazzier varieties.

planted this particular flower simply because it's beautiful. Instead, we choose tulips with the kind of careful consideration that we give to the interior decoration of our homes, because, subconsciously or not, we want them to make a statement about who we are.

Recently, for example, subdued shades in tulips (and in most flowers, for that matter) had great snob appeal. Gardeners "in the know" shunned brassy tulip varieties in colors like fire-engine red or orange or magenta, even though these were highly popular in the 1960s. Striped, flamed or fringy kinds of tulips, which made the early Dutch dizzy with delight, got the cold shoulder too. ("How I hate those gaudy Parrot tulips" was a common cry of "discerning" gardeners during the 1990s.) That's because admitting to a penchant for stridently hued varieties marked you instantly as a bit of a rube, the kind of gardener who went in for white plastic flowerpots and garden gnomes.

Instead, gardeners announced to other gardeners how classy they were by choosing tulips in "tasteful" colors: pale pinks and yellows, violets and apricot. To be even classier, they selected really dark hues, like brick red or plum. It's no surprise that a variety of tulip called 'Queen of Night' achieved almost cult status in the last decade of the twentieth century. Its maroon-black, velvety petals were perceived to denote opulence and sophistication—and everybody wanted to show that they possessed both.

RED RAVE: *Around the world, the most popular tulip color is red. This one is* T. greigii *'Red Torch.'*

Now the pendulum is starting to swing back. While "black" tulips remain all the rage, many of us, it seems, are getting tired of wishy-washy hues. Influenced by a few outspoken gardening gurus, like Britain's Christopher Lloyd (who is fond of saying "a pox on all these dishwater colors"), gardeners are getting adventurous again. As part of that trend, vividly colored tulips have hit the comeback trail. Like Impressionist painter Claude Monet, Lloyd adores red and yellow tulips; he plants hundreds of them in his garden at Great Dixter, England. Lloyd's taste for brilliant color combinations—and the bold approach to gardening taken by other trend-setters in North America and Europe—is persuading people everywhere to abandon the subdued-shades-only mantra of the 1980s and 1990s.

Becoming popular again are yellow tulips, particularly several shades of yellow combined. The same thing is happening to orange varieties, and to stripy, two-tone blooms. Gardeners are, in fact, becoming passionate once more about the exotic, hit-you-in-the-eye colors that in bygone days entranced everybody from Turkish sultans to French kings, and turned tulips into the most popular flowers in the world.

It's about time.

How to grow tulips successfully

Tulips aren't particularly fussy about soil, but they have two essential requirements. One is good drainage. The other is sun—they like lots of it. In claylike soil that holds water, these kinds of bulbs are prone to fungal

PICTURE PERFECT: *A backyard bursting with glorious tulips isn't difficult to achieve, as long as you plan it the previous fall.*

diseases, which make them rot. And in a shady location, tulip stems often get so long and leggy, they will collapse in a spaghetti-like mess—or produce disappointingly few flowers. (Parrot varieties are particularly prone to do this. They need at least six hours of sun a day, and a sheltered location.)

If soil is on the heavy side, adding a good dollop of sand (that's coarse, gritty sand, not the fine stuff) will help. In fact, sandy soil suits tulips to a T, which is hardly surprising when you consider that they come from the dry, stony steppes of Central Asia. Nowadays, in Holland, they are raised in the kind of soil that one bulb supplier describes as "a beach with a bit of loam mixed into it." If you can duplicate that effect in your garden, so much the better. Besides sand, it's a good idea to work in plenty of compost and peat moss.

THAT DRATTED BULB FOLIAGE

It looks messy. It gets in the way. But ...

When tulips have finished blooming, nip off their spent flower heads at the top of the stems, but don't be tempted to get out the garden shears. The bulbs down below will thank you (by sending up more flowers next year) if you let stems and leaves wither naturally. Both are needed to send nourishment down to the bulb. The time to get rid of them is when they've gone brown and come out of the ground easily, after a gentle tug.

Vexed that decaying tulip foliage takes up too much space—and looks awful—some neatnik gardeners plait the leaves and stems and pin them to the ground, behind other plants. ("Please don't!" wail the bulb experts.) Or they undertake a complicated ritual: the tulip bulbs are dug up after

BYE BYE BLOOMS: Tulip heads should be snipped off after flowering. This is called "deadheading." But leave bulb foliage to die down naturally.

blooming, then replanted in a tucked-away spot in the garden and left there until the foliage has withered away completely; after that (it usually takes about six weeks), these zealous souls dig up the bulbs once more, dry them off on racks and replant them in the original flower bed. This is certainly an option, if you have tons of time for all that digging and drying. If you don't, simply plunk a flowerpot of colorful annuals in front of the decaying foliage. Or, even better, interplant tulips with late-appearing perennials that will shoot up leaves and stems, masking the bulbs' detritus. (*Sedum spectabile* and *Hostas* are both good choices.) For, all things considered, it really works better just to leave tulips where they are.

Unappealing bulb foliage is—as garden writer Thalassa Cruso points out—a burden that philosophical gardeners learn to put up with. "I control my itching hands which long to pull these miseries [the bulb stems and leaves] out," she writes in *The Gardening Year.* "Instead, I let them remain like bleached bones in a desert, the ghosts of plants that have been—and the token of flowers that will be."

DEFINITELY EYECATCHING: T. greigii *'Rockery Master' has short stems and is ideal for the front of a flower border.*

Contrary to advice dished out in many gardening books, the end of fall is a perfectly acceptable time to plant tulips. For compared with other spring bulbs, tulips have one great advantage: they don't mind if you procrastinate. Daffodils demand that you get busy in September; tulips will wait. It's actually a good idea to get other fall gardening chores done first, because you can delay putting in your tulips until winter is starting to make its presence felt (but don't leave it so long that the ground is frozen and you have to hack holes with a pickax). In most areas of North America, tulips can be safely planted throughout November. Be sure to pick spots where the sun will hit the ground next spring. In fact, sit down and consider the chosen location carefully. While it's great to provide a show that will thrill neighbors and people passing on the street, don't you also want to locate some tulips where you can delight in their beauty yourself, from inside the house?

Most gardening books advise digging individual holes for tulips, using a gadget called a dibber, but this is actually not the best way to plant them.

That's because, once the flowers come up in spring, they tend to have a "dib-dobbed" look—the result of being spaced too far apart. What works better for tulips (which are quite small compared with many other bulbs) is excavating a shallow pit. This pit can extend over a large area, if you want a big swath of blooms, or be quite small, if you're just planting a few tulips in a clump.

FORMULA TO FOLLOW: Three times as deep as the bulb is high is the planting depth recommended by bulb experts.

Planting depth also isn't as crucial as gardening books claim, but you need to dig out at least 6"/15 cm in most areas (more if you live in northern regions). A good ratio is three times as deep as the bulb is high. If you have some sand, sprinkle a bit over the entire excavated area, then arrange the tulip bulbs on top—3"/8 cm apart, not 8"/20 cm as advocated by many experts. (Small species tulips can be massed even closer together, and they don't have to be planted as deep as hybrid tulips.) Don't put the bulbs in rows unless you're after a deliberately geometric pattern.

If it's not possible to excavate a pit, due to tree root and plants being tangled up together in the flower bed, tuck tulip bulbs in anywhere you can make holes. (Species tulips are remarkably adept at settling in anywhere, so long as there's adequate drainage.) Make sure the pointed end of the bulb is facing upwards. Press the bulb firmly into the ground, then throw soil back on top of everything and press it down. In areas with really harsh winters, add a layer of leaves or some evergreen branches on top.

Water well and start dreaming of spring.

Tulips can also be grown in pots or window boxes, but it's a little more complicated. Follow the same planting procedure—that is, pot up the bulbs in the fall, in a good growing medium. Then these containers must be stored in a garage or shed for three months in *total* darkness before bringing them out into the light. (See "The fun of forcing," page 96.)

What's simpler, however, when you want potted tulips out of doors is to wait till spring, and then buy pre-sprouted tulip bulblets from a garden center. These are now available in many locations, and you treat them in the same way as flats of annuals. Pot up the bulblets (pick plants that have short stems and tightly closed buds) in large containers, filled with a good growing mix that doesn't retain water. Get them acclimatized to the outdoors in a shady area for the first few days. Then put the pots out on your balcony, terrace or whatever, and they'll look as good as any tulips planted in a regular garden.

What to do in warmer climates

Unlike humans, tulips actually crave cold winters. A period of freezing is necessary for the bulbs to develop properly under the ground. That's what makes them difficult to grow in areas where the weather stays mild from November through March.

Generally speaking, USDA Zone 8 is the southern limit for planting tulips in gardens. However, some intrepid souls in USDA Zones 9 and 10 do manage to enjoy a springtime fix of these flowers by indulging in a bit of trickery.

To try it, don't plant tulip bulbs in the ground during the fall; instead, give them the cold treatment in a refrigerator. Store bulbs in a ventilated bag (made of paper or mesh, not plastic—discarded onion bags do the job admirably) for at least six to eight weeks, but preferably three months, at the usual refrigerator temperature (40–45°F/ 5–7°C). It's a good idea to set aside an old fridge for this purpose, as you can't store any fruit (especially apples) or tomatoes in there at the same time as the tulips. Fruit gives off an ethylene gas that kills bulbs.

Keep the tulips in the fridge (or a room that's really cool) until the moment you want to put them in the ground. Plant in December or early

PASTEL PERFECTION: *Lily-flowered 'China Pink,' an early bloomer, combines well with grape hyacinths (*muscari) *and* narcissus.

January, about 6"/15 cm deep, and cover with a two-inch layer of mulch to keep things cool and moist. Water regularly—and keep your fingers crossed.

These tulips are recommended for warmer climates:

- Single late varieties, such as 'Halcro' (vibrant red); 'Queen of Night' (maroon-black); 'Renown' (rose pink); 'Menton' (apricot pink with an inside of poppy red); and 'Hocus Pocus' (yellow tipped with pink).

- Single early varieties such as 'Apricot Beauty' (soft salmon pink) and, in the Triumph category, 'New Design' (yellow fading to pinkish white).

ADAPTABLE: 'Halcro,' a single late tulip, is one variety recommended for warmer climates.

- Tougher varieties of Darwin tulips, such as 'Apeldoorn' (red) and 'Golden Apeldoorn' (yellow).

- Species tulips such as *Linifolia* (red); *Tarda* (yellow and white); *Saxatilis* (lavender with yellow); and *Bakeri* 'Lilac Wonder.' These types of tulips can sometimes even be grown in warmer climates without precooling— and may multiply well by themselves.

WHEN JACK FROST PAYS A RETURN VISIT

Should we cover tulips up during an unexpected cold snap? Generally speaking, no. Spring-flowering bulbs are tough. They can usually take what Mother Nature dishes out. Don't be tempted to tamper with them if the weather suddenly gets warm, then cold again.

That word comes from the Netherlands Flower Bulb Information Center in New York City. This organization gets thousands of calls and e-mails every spring from panicky gardeners wondering what to do when the temperature plummets unexpectedly. "People think they should cover up their tulips with mulch if it's going to snow or freeze overnight," says director Sally Ferguson. "But it's better to just leave them alone."

TOUGH GUYS: If there's a sudden cold snap, leave tulips to cope by themselves. Covering them up will bruise flowers and tender stems.

Tulips planted in a garden will automatically stop growing when cold weather returns. While emerging closed buds and leaves may look a bit "pinched," they aren't harmed by Jack Frost's icy grip. In fact, what hurts them far more is gardeners hastily laying out mulches of leaves and blankets, because tender young plants get bruised easily.

However, there are exceptions. Pre-sprouted bulblets, raised in a nursery and planted in the garden in spring, don't take kindly to sudden drops in temperature. Nor do tulips planted in pots; the edges of their petals are prone to "freezer burn" and won't recover. In both instances, if it looks like cold weather is on the way, cut the flowers off and bring them indoors; enjoy their beauty in a vase—or remove the entire pot to a warmer location.

The fun of forcing

There's one trouble with tulips: they make us wait—and wait—for their brief bursts of glory. After planting them, often with frozen fingers, in the fall, many a gardener has stared out the window, impatiently drumming those digits. It always seems so unbearably long before winter ends and we get to see the glorious results of all that hard work!

If you aren't good at the waiting game, there is an alternative. Try forcing.

"Forcing" is a rather unpleasant-sounding term that's used to describe the highly satisfying procedure by which plants are persuaded to bloom before their normal flowering period. Nurseries do it as a matter of course. Back in Victorian times, people loved to make all kinds of flowers bloom early. Nowadays, most of us tend to think it's too complicated, which is a shame; for where spring bulbs are concerned, forcing a few in a pot is surprisingly simple, as long as you follow a few rules.

Tulips, generally speaking, don't force as well as other spring-flowering bulbs (such as hyacinths and daffodils). For success, the trick is to pick single, early-blooming varieties with shorter stems. Varieties that bloom later in the spring mostly have long stems, which tend to get leggy and sprawl unattractively when planted in pots.

Among single early tulips, 'Apricot Beauty' is an inspired choice because it's both beautiful (with pale pinkish-orange flowers) and smells nice indoors. Shorter-stemmed Triumph tulips, such as 'Los Angeles' (signal red edged with bright yellow) and 'Prinses Irene' (orange with a purple flame), are also recommended for forcing. One bulb expert suggests that beginners try forcing species tulips, particularly *kaufmanniana* and *greigii*. Although their flowers aren't as showy as the hybrid tulips, he says they will produce an attractive display with little trouble.

Whatever the tulip that's being coaxed into blooming indoors in winter, the planting

WINTER ENTERTAINMENT: A pot of forced tulips is a marvelous morale booster for both pets and people.

procedure is the same. Choose a small pot (say 6″/15 cm in diameter), because forced bulbs look best planted close together. Fill it to within 2″/5 cm of the top with a good potting soil mixed with a bit of bulb fertilizer. Put the bulbs in, nudging up to one another but not touching, with the flat side of each bulb facing the outside of the pot. (Tulips throw their first, and largest, leaf to that side, and you want it to be on the outside, not the inside, of the container.) Fill in more soil around the bulbs. Make sure the bulbs are pointing upwards, with their snouts protruding from the soil.

SHOW OF FORCE: Species tulips like these are often easier to force indoors than hybrid varieties.

If you're a balcony gardener wanting to pot up a window box full of tulips, the planting procedure is basically the same—but you'll need dozens of bulbs. (Bear in mind, too, that this window box is going to have to be stored inside a garage or shed till next spring. Once it's filled with soil, such an object can get mighty heavy to haul around.)

Whatever the container, water well and put it in complete darkness, at a temperature of about 40°F/4°C. There should be no danger of freezing in the chosen location. A cupboard in a garage is often a good bet, but it should have ventilation holes (or leave the cupboard door open a crack), because without air the pot will acquire a layer of mold. A refrigerator on the coolest setting works well too, but remember that you can't store fruit in the fridge at the same time (it gives off ethylene gas, which will kill the tulips).

FORCING CALENDAR:

- To have tulips blooming in January, pot up bulbs in September or very early October.
- For flowers in February, pot up in early to mid-October.
- For flowers in March, pot up in late October or early November.

Keep the soil moist but not wet. After about three months, check. Little sprouts—hallelujah!—should be appearing. Move the pot to a warmer location (about 65°F/18°C), but still keep it dark. Wait till the sprouts have grown a couple more inches, then introduce the pot gradually into normal daylight. A dimly lit room works best for the first week or two. (Window boxes should simply be hauled out of the dark in early spring and placed outside when the weather is starting to warm up.)

After adjusting to the brightness, forced tulips are ready to strut their stuff on the dining table, window ledge or wherever. Tight buds will come up, then gradually open up into luscious flowers—a truly thrilling sight that's a perfect antidote to the blahs of February. (Keep the room on the cool side and the flowers will last longer.) In fact, when the world outside is still in the grip of winter, the not-very-difficult act of bringing tulips into bloom indoors is so uplifting, you'll wonder why you didn't try the fun of forcing before.

COMBATING CRITTERS:

Every spring and fall on gardening hotlines across North America, people frantically call up with the same question: "How can I stop squirrels digging up/nibbling/destroying my tulips?"

The short answer is (sigh), you can't. Not completely. There is, sad to say, no 100-percent foolproof way to outwit those pesky little bushy-tails and other critters, like mice, moles, voles and skunks. Nor can you deter deer who are intent upon helping themselves to tulip munchies. However, here are a few environmentally friendly deterrents that sometimes work:

DO

- Plant bulbs really deep (say 10″/25 cm). Add prickly holly leaves or pieces of thistle to the planting holes. (If you do plant deep, remember that the tulips will take longer to appear the following spring.)

- Wrap tulip bulbs in chicken wire or wide-mesh black plastic netting when you plant them. Don't worry about the mesh inhibiting growth: tulip leaves and flower stems will poke their way through it.

- Give bulbs a suit of armor. Encase them in old coffee cans, with wire netting or hardware cloth spread on top and secured around the sides of the can with a piece of wire. Be sure to punch holes in the sides and bottom of the can.

- Smooth out the area where you planted the tulips. Squirrels are more likely to go digging where soil looks disturbed.

- Stick sharp bamboo barbecue skewers into the soil all over the area where the tulips are. (This deters domestic kitties too.)

HIDDEN ASSETS: Spiky, yellow-bloomed Fritillaria Imperialis *center, behind the tulips) emits a powerful, skunky smell that squirrels hate. Planted with tulips, it may keep the critters away.*

- Plant a tall flowering bulb called Crown Imperial (*Fritillaria imperialis*) together with your tulip bulbs. It has a skunky smell that squirrels hate. You can also try interplanting the bulbs with cloves of garlic.

- When flowers come up in spring, spray them with a garlic-and-water solution. Repeat after it rains.

- Get a dog or cat. Their presence is sometimes sufficient to scare squirrels off.

- Try sprinkling blood meal where you planted the bulbs. (It does deter squirrels, but unfortunately, dogs and cats like munching on it.)

- To deter deer, try the urine of their predators—wolves and coyotes— placed in special containers around the garden. Several companies now sell these devices by mail order.

DON'T

- Add bone meal to the planting hole. (Squirrels and other animals go digging for it.) A commercial bulb fertilizer is less likely to attract unwelcome visitors.

- Plant tulips around trees where squirrels hibernate in winter.

- Use mothballs (they're toxic to pets) or hot pepper, which can blind squirrels and cause them incredible pain. (Animal protection societies now frown upon this practice.)

TERRIFIC TULIP COMBINATIONS

Tulips of different colors look great together. For a bold, in-your-face effect, try combining red and yellow, or yellow and purple, or burgundy and orange. For a subtler impact, choose softer shades: pinks, violets and purples. Or keep it simple with plain white.

One current "hot" trend in garden design, according to experts on both sides of the Atlantic, is to combine two different hues of the same color. Try mixing a mass of bright yellow tulips with others in a shade of deep gold. Or juxtapose a variety that's pale pink against one that's magenta.

Tulips also harmonize happily with many other spring flowers. A few combinations to try:

- 'Étude,' which is blood-red edged in canary yellow, and saffron-hued 'Paul Richter' with wallflowers (*Erysimum cheiri*) in the same striking red and yellow shades; purple 'Negrita' tulips with white violas; 'Prinses Irene' tulips, whose petals are several shades of orange, with orangey-red 'Fire King' wallflowers (*Erysimum cheiri*); pink-and-white-striped 'Sorbet' tulips with blue-and-white forget-me-nots (*Myosotis*);

MONET'S FAVORITES: *The Impressionist painter loved red and yellow tulips planted together. This combination was also very popular in the 1950s.*

UNABASHEDLY BRIGHT: Monet loved bold tulips like this parrot variety.

pink-streaked 'Angélique' double tulips and 'Esther,' a cherry pink single variety, under-planted with red and mauve pansies.

These kinds of combinations were all favorites of Impressionist painter Claude Monet, who was unabashed in his use of bold hues. At Monet's garden in Giverny, outside Paris, you can still see such color schemes blooming in March and April.

- Scarlet and/or bright yellow tulips (any early-blooming variety; the tough-as-nails 'Apel-doorn' and 'Golden Apeldoorn' are recommended) with common Spurge (*Euphorbia polychroma*), an easy-to-grow shrubby plant that has acid yel-low-green flowers.

- 'Greenland' (or 'Groenland') tulips with common bleeding heart (*Dicentra spectabile*) is an easy-to-grow combination that looks stunning. Sometimes known as the watermelon tulip, 'Greenland' has pink-and-white petals with a green stripe running through the center. Its three col-ors mimic exactly the dainty flowers and leaves of the bleeding heart.

For a variation on this theme, try white bleeding heart (*Dicentra spectabile* 'Alba') with one of the following tulips: lily-flowered 'White Triumphator'; green-streaked Viridiflora 'Spring Green'; or 'Black Parrot.'

- A long, dramatic sweep of tulips in analogous colors—that is, shades that are all on the same side of the color wheel. Pick a selection of tulips in yellows, oranges and golds. For a swath in pinks and reds, start with white, then go to pale pinks, followed by magenta and purpley red, finishing with the deep maroon-black of 'Queen of Night.'

WONDERFUL WHITES: *Lily-flowered 'White Triumphator'* looks gorgeous combined with white bleeding heart Dicentra spectabile *'Alba.'*

(You need a big flower bed to do this; and be sure to pick varieties that all bloom at the same time.)

- Species tulip *T. batalinii*, which is a soft yellow, with any lavender-colored Aubrieta or violet *Phlox divaricata*. Both of the latter plants form cushions, through which tulip stems poke prettily.

- Another species tulip, *T. clusiana*, which is red, underplanted with a creeping form of the herb rosemary, *R. eriocalyx* 'Prostratus.' This was a favorite combination of the famous British gardener Vita Sackville-West.

six

𝒯ulips à la carte: Food Fun, Flower Arranging and More

Anyone for Tulip Tetrazzini?

Believe it or not, you can eat tulips. Other springtime bulbs (such as daffodils) are poisonous to animals and humans, but the bulbs of tulips actually taste good, according to some people. "They're like onions, but with a less pronounced flavor," says one North American bulb expert, who fried up a few once in butter, out of curiosity.

MASTERFUL MINIMALISM: Arranging tulips this way is a hot trend. Pick flowers in plain colors. Place only one bloom in each glass bottle or vase.

FORGET THE FLOWERS: Tulip blooms like T. greigii *'Oriental Beauty' enchant us today. But back in the sixteenth century, their underpinnings often had more allure. Wealthy people ate tulip bulbs—and treated them as aphrodisiacs.*

This adventurous woman isn't the first person to make a meal out of Holland's most famous flower export. During World War II, many Dutch citizens avoided starvation by raiding the tulip fields. Further back, in the sixteenth century, when tulips were first introduced to Europe from Turkey, some people even treated the bulbs as an exotic new vegetable. They ate them, boiled or roasted, with oil and vinegar. According to one account, a Flemish merchant found a bag of bulbs wrapped up inside a shipment of

TOMATOES À LA TULIPE

Tulip bulbs can be substituted for onions in any recipe. For a tomato sauce, slice two bulbs and sauté them in olive oil with a little garlic. Add four cups of peeled, chopped tomatoes and simmer for about half an hour. Add a chopped herb of your choice, such as parsley or basil. Serve over pasta, with Parmesan cheese.

The stamens and ovaries of tulip flowers have a taste similar to asparagus. Steam them, or sauté in butter.

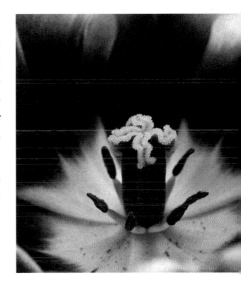

LIKE ASPARAGUS: *What's inside the tulip can actually be cooked and eaten.*

carpets from Constantinople. So he chowed down on a few for dinner, then planted the rest in his garden, anticipating more "Turkish onions" in spring. When gorgeous flowers came up instead, the fellow got the surprise of his life.

Others got far worse. Horror stories abound about Dutch citizens dining on tulip bulbs—only to discover later that what they'd consigned to their stomachs was the equivalent of a winning lottery ticket today. This supposedly happened during the giddy years of Tulipomania (1623–37), when single tulip bulbs sold for astronomical sums. Although the merchant classes were aware of the bulbs' value, and competed crazily for them, a lot of ordinary Dutch men and women weren't. As a result, someone might, by chance, acquire a few bulbs and, because they looked like onions, turn them into a meal by mistake.

Whether this actually happened, or whether tales about tulips got embroidered over the years, is anyone's guess. However, fact or fiction, British author Deborah Moggach included such an incident in her best-selling 1999 novel *Tulip Fever*. In this steamy tale (made into a movie by Steven Spielberg), Gerrit, the drunken manservant, is dispatched by artist Jan to pick up several packages. One contains a solitary tulip. Jan intends selling this valuable specimen so that he and his married lover, who is pregnant with their child, can flee Amsterdam. However, after a boozing session at the pub, Gerrit, not clued in by Jan, slices up the "onion" and enjoys it for lunch, with pickled herring. Disaster ensues.

Across the Channel, upper-class Brits began nibbling on the bulbs too, as the fashion for tulips spread to England during the reign of Elizabeth I. They in fact became the beluga caviar of the day, a sophisticated delicacy available only to those who could afford their high price. One enthusiast described the bulbs as "firme and sound, fit to be presented to the curious." There were even whispers that they had Viagra-like powers. "I cannot say either from my selfe, not having eaten many … if there are any special properties," wrote one gentleman cautiously to another, "… but I think they may well have it."

An English botanist, John Parkinson, came to the conclusion that the usefulness of tulips extended not below the belt but above it. He

HOW TO CANDY TULIP PETALS

Use only tulips that you have grown, and that have come up for the second season in your garden. (These bulbs will no longer carry any traces of pesticides.) Since tulip petals' taste can vary according to the soil in which the bulbs were planted, nibble on one first to see if you like the flavor.

Pick flower heads in the early morning. Pull petals off carefully, so they aren't bruised. Dip petals in lightly beaten egg white and shake off any excess. Lay them on a cookie sheet spread with a layer of fine sugar. Coat the petals with sugar on both sides.

recommended mashing tulip petals into red wine, to cure "a cricke in the necke."

Modern males aren't inclined to chomp on tulip bulbs before a hot date. Nor do we toss them into a stir-fry (there's surely no point, when onions are so cheap) or glug down their petals with the Gamay Noir. However, this perennially popular plant is evolving yet again, in the twenty-first century, into a sought-after food experience for the elite. This time, though, it's the bloom, not the bulb. As palates get jaded by the likes

STRANGE REMEDY: *Three hundred years ago, a British botanist insisted on mashing tulip petals like these into red wine. He said they cured "a cricke in the necke."*

of nasturtiums, pansies and squash blossoms, the fashion for edible flowers is turning to tulips—in many guises.

On the west coast (where food fads tend to blossom first), buds, single petals and whole tulips, carefully sliced, are appearing on the menu in upscale restaurants. At the Fairmont Waterfront Hotel in Vancouver, British Columbia, you can, during the spring tulip season, feast on tulip blossoms dipped in tempura batter. Or a red tulip and green bean salad. Or lightly sautéed green tulip buds. For dessert, the hotel wraps things up with candied pink tulip petals, served over ice cream.

One lifestyle magazine suggested recently that tulip flower heads, stuffed with cream cheese and chives, would make perfect hors d'oeuvres for an elegant dinner party.

The Japanese can already buy candied tulip petals in supermarkets. Perhaps it won't be long before we're doing the same thing.

Tips on arranging tulips

Tulips make lovely cut flowers. However, they have one drawback: they tend to get the droops. After a few hours in a vase their stems often bend over, and the blooms hang downwards, so you can't see them properly. That's because the stems have soaked up water, sitting in the vase. To circumvent this annoying occurrence, try a trick used by professional floral arrangers: roll tulips tightly in damp newspaper (the paper should extend above the flower tops but not cover the lower third of the stems), then

STRAIGHT AND TALL: *One way to stop cut tulips getting the droops is to arrange them inside a glass vase.*

leave them standing in cool water, in a tall container, for a couple of hours before putting them into a vase.

Properly cared for, cut tulips should last five to eight days after their buds open. They adapt well to all kinds of floral displays. Arrange them solo (their sculptured shapes are great on their own), or mix them with other spring flowers and foliage.

For a minimalist look on a tabletop or window ledge, try a trio of classically shaped tulips in a row of three glass bottles. Choose plain-colored blooms, like white, yellow, red or a deep purple.

For a more exotic, hey-look-at-me arrangement, try the latest craze: parrot tulips. These are sometimes called "leaf lettuces in Technicolor" because their frilly shapes and brilliant colors are so striking. A bunch of parrots, in different colors, will perk up any room. Professional floral arrangers are big fans of these types of tulips. (So were Dutch painters in the sixteenth century.) They recommend: 'Orange Favorite' (orange mixed with green); 'Flaming Parrot' (yellow streaked with red); 'Estella Rijnveld' (cherry red flamed with white); and 'Black Parrot' (deep purple-black). Choose a plain vase to display them.

> It's amazing but true: tulip stems go on growing—often as much as 3"/8 cm —after they've been cut.

Other pointers from the pros:

- When buying bunches of tulips, look for buds that are still closed but about to open. They should show the color of the flower.

- Go for colors with oomph. Don't be wishy-washy. But pick a vase that won't clash, or compete, with the flowers.

- Remove leaves and the bottom inch or two of the stems, cutting diagonally with a clean, sharp knife.

- Don't waste money on those little packets of "floral conditioner." And forget old wives' tales about putting Aspirins or pennies in the vase. Cut tulips are satisfied with plain water. Just make sure you top it up daily.

- Place the vase in a cool spot if you want the flowers to last.

- Don't mix daffodils in a vase with tulips. The daffodils will release a slimy substance that kills the tulips.

- Once you've arranged the flowers, peel back a few tulip petals to show the stamens inside. This adds interest.

- Expect your arrangement to change its shape a bit. Tulips will bend crazily towards the light, so turn the vase regularly.

HEY LOOK AT ME: *Like all parrot tulips, 'Orange Favorite' is an inspired choice for floral arrangements.*

Growing your own cut tulips

The choice of cut tulips in florists' shops and supermarkets used to be boring—just a few plain colors, like white, pink and yellow. That's because tulips for the cut-flower market were grown in few places. Now, however, they are raised extensively in both Holland and North America (some are also imported from South America), and it's not hard to see why. Americans buy a staggering number of cut tulips: more than 83 million every year. Responding to the demand, growers are making the selection less limited. You can now find cut tulips with red and white stripes in supermarkets, and sometimes even frilly, flamboyant Parrots in riotous colors.

For the best selection, however, consider setting aside some space in the garden to grow your own. Choose varieties that bloom in sequence, so there's something to cut throughout the spring. Also, plant a lot of them. That way you won't be worried about getting out the scissors and bringing bunches of them indoors, once they start to bloom.

These tulips are recommended as cutting flowers: 'Prinses Irene' Triumph (early, a vibrant orange with a base of purple); 'Mickey Mouse' (single early, in a zingy red and yellow); 'Queen

GREAT FOR CUTTING: Cream and green petals of Viridiflora 'Spring Green' blend well with other colors.

of Night' (single late, maroon-purple, a perfect backdrop for other flowers); Viridiflora 'Spring Green' (cream-and-green petals that look different and combine well with other blooms); and lily-flowered varieties such as 'White Triumphator,' 'Aladdin' and 'Ballerina' (the graceful, urn-like shape adds a touch of elegance). As a bonus, 'Ballerina' is fragrant.

Making tulips last—in the microwave

Tulips look so terrific indoors, it's a shame their beauty is fleeting. After a brief few days of glory in a vase, the petals start to drop and they're ready for the garbage can. For a permanent display, try a new idea that's come along recently: pressing tulips in the microwave.

Some types of tulips, particularly the smaller species tulips, take surprisingly well to being dried in this fashion. Parrot tulips are also a good bet, because they retain their brilliant colors.

To microwave tulips, you need: 2 pieces of plywood about 10″ × 8″/25 cm × 20 cm (or any size that you can comfortably turn in the microwave); some thick elastics, about 1/4″/50 mm wide; and 6 pieces of blotting paper.

Shake pollen off the tulip. Trim the stem. Set out one piece of plywood (shiny side outside), covered with three pieces of blotting paper. Arrange the tulip blooms you want to press on top. Try peeling a couple of petals back to make an attractive display but don't do too many at once. Lay more blotting paper and the other sheet of plywood on top. Press firmly shut. If it feels lumpy, lay a weight on top for a while, or stand on it.

Place elastics around this "sandwich" and microwave on medium heat for two minutes. Don't be tempted to use full power; high heat will frizzle the flowers. Remove, but DON'T look inside yet (it's hot!). Put something heavy on top, like telephone directories, until the sandwich is completely cool. Open carefully and remove the tulip, using tweezers. If the bloom isn't completely dry, repeat the process. (You may need to use fresh elastics, as they often get wrecked in the microwave.)

Combine microwaved tulips with other springtime flowers (dried using

the same process) in a framed "collage." Or place them under a sheet of glass on a coffee table. An arrangement of tulips on a piece of burlap, framed, makes a great Christmas gift.

FOREVER FANTASTIC: Parrot tulips like 'Feathered Beauty' dry well in the microwave, because they retain their brilliant colors.

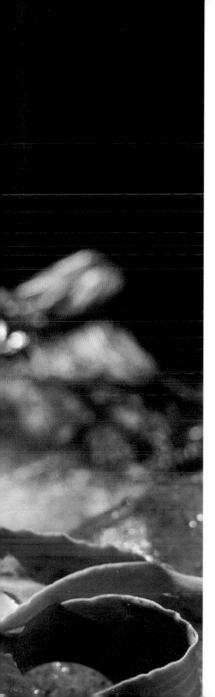

seven

*W*here to Buy Tulips

Two web sites offer a wealth of information about tulips:

www.bulb.com
Operated by the Netherlands Flower Bulb Information Center, this is an excellent resource. Well laid out and easy to navigate, it has everything you need to know about growing tulips and where to buy them. They don't sell bulbs.

www.tulipworld.com
An on-line company, operated from Amsterdam, that won an award from the Garden Writers

TAKE YOUR PICK: There are thousands of different tulips and dozens of places to buy them. This stripy-leafed stunner is T. greigii *'Marianne.'*

Association of America. It's fun to navigate, offers plenty of information and sells a variety of spring-flowering bulbs. Tulipworld is one of the few places where you can buy Eco Tulips—bulbs raised without the use of pesticides. (Bear in mind, however, that European regulations regarding pesticide use are far stricter than those in North America, and that all flowering bulbs carry only trace amounts of chemicals.)

The following is a list of companies that sell tulip bulbs to consumers.

United States

Ambrose Gardens
Roseville, MN
651-917-0090
Specializes in bulbs for Zones 3 and 4.

Bloomingbulb
Medford, OR
541-772-2908

Borbeleta Gardens
Fairbault, MN
507-334-2807

Breck's Dutch Bulbs
Peoria, IL
800-722-9069

Brent & Becky's Bulbs
Gloucester, VA
877-661-2852

Bulb Barn
Fair Lawn, NJ
201-794-4704

The Bulb Crate
Riverwoods, IL
847-317-1414

Bundles of Bulbs
New Hope, PA
877-986-2852

W. Atlee Burpee
Warminster, PA
800-888-1447

Colorblends
Greenwich, CT
888-847-8637

Dirk Visser's Holland Bulbs
Ipswich, MA
800-582-3650

Dutch Gardens
Adelphia, NJ
800-818-3861

Ferry Morse Seeds
Fulton, KY
800-283-3400

French's Bulb Importers
Pittsfield, VT
800-286-8198

Geerlings Bulbs USA
Babylon, NY
On-line bulb ordering.

Gurney Seed
Yankton, SD
605-665-9310

Harris Seeds
Rochester, NY
800-514-4441

Henry Field's Seed & Nursery Co
Grand Rapids, MI
616-453-5401

House of Wesley Nursery
Bloomington, IL
309-663-9551

Jackson & Perkins
Medford, OR
800-854-6200

J.W. Jung Seed Co.
Randolph, WI
800-247-5864

Martha by Mail
800-950-7130

McClure & Zimmerman
Friesland, WI
800-883-6998

Messelaar Bulb Co.
Ipswich, MA
978-356-3737

Michigan Bulb Co.
Grand Rapids, MI
800-340-7749

Mueller, Charles H.
New Hope, PA
888-594-2852

Netherland Bulb Co.
Easton, PA
800-755-2852

Odyssey Bulbs
Berrien Springs, MI
616-471-4642
Hard-to-find varieties.

Old House Gardens/Heirloom
  Bulbs
Ann Arbor, MI
734-995-1486
Antique/heritage bulbs.

Park Seed Co.
Greenwood, SC
800-845-3369

Planetgarden.com
Norcross, GA
On-line source of bulbs.

Roozengaarde
Mt. Vernon, WA
800-732-3266

Scheepers, John
Bantam, CT
860-567-0838

Spring Hill Nurseries
Peoria, IL
800-544-0294

Territorial Seed Co.
Cottage Grove, OR
541-942-9547

Thomas Jefferson Center for
   Historic Plants
Monticello, Charlottesville, VA
www.monticello.org
*Specializes in flowering bulbs that
Jefferson grew.*

Thompson & Morgan
Jackson, NJ
800-274-7333

Van Bourgondien Bros.
Babylon, NY
800-622-9997

Van Dycks Flower Farms
Brightwaters, NY
800-248-2852

Van Engelen
Litchfield, CT
860-567-8734

Vanveen Bulbs International
Estacada, OR
888-289-2852

Veldheer Tulip Gardens
Holland, MI
616-399-1900

Wayside Gardens
Hodges, SC
800-845-1124

We-Du Nurseries
Marion, NC
828-738-8300

White Flower Farms
Litchfield, CT
800-503-9624

Wooden Shoe Bulb Co.
Mt. Angel, OR
800-711-2006
www.woodenshoe.com
*More than 160 tulip varieties,
mostly homegrown.*

Canada

Aimers
Aurora, Ontario
905-833-0282

Botanus
Langley, B.C.
800-672-3413

Cruickshanks
Toronto, Ontario
800-665-5605
www.indigo.ca

Dominion Seed House
Georgetown, Ontario
905-873-3037

Gardenimport Inc.
Thornhill, Ontario
905-731-1950
www.gardenimport.com
Unusual varieties of flowering bulbs.

Horticlub
Laval, Quebec
450-682-9071

McConnell Nurseries
Strathroy, Ontario
800-363-0901

McFadyen Seed Co.
Brandon, Manitoba
800-363-0901

Vesey's Seeds
York, P.E.I.
800-686-0329
www.veseys.com
Wide selection of tulips.

Victoria Flower & Bulb Warehouse
Victoria, B.C.
www.victoriaflowerandbulb.com

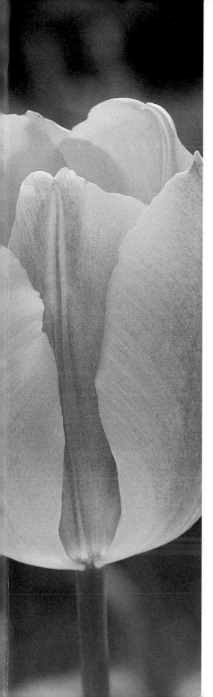

$\mathscr{A}$cknowledgments

The author wishes to thank Carol Cowan of the Netherlands Flower Bulb Information Centre, Toronto, for her guidance, patience and infinite knowledge about tulips. Thanks are also extended to: Mara Arndt, Civic Garden Centre, Toronto; Dugald Cameron, Gardenimport, Ontario; Peggy Cornett, Director, Thomas Jefferson Center for Historic Plants, Virginia; Susan Day, art historian, Paris; Josephine Felton, tulip lover, Gloucestershire, England; Michel Gauthier and Doug Little, Ottawa Tulip Festival; the Iverson family, Wooden Shoe Bulb Company, Mount Angel, Oregon; and editor, Janice Zawerbny.